PUNK
PSYCHOLOGY

Keith Scott-Mumby MD, MB ChB, HMD, PhD

Published by:
Supernoetics® Inc.
PO Box 371225, Las Vegas, NV 89137

10 9 8 7 6 5 4 3 2 1

ISBN 978-0-9990521-0-5

US Library Of Congress listing applied for.

CONTENTS

1. Introducing Hypnoetics™ 11

2. "Real" IQ 21

3. The Scale Of Emotional and Social Health 33

4. A Brief History Of Mind Exploration 47

5. What Is A Mind? 61

6. How Does It Go Wrong? 73

7. Terminology And Structures 85

8. What We Are Doing In Piloting 103

9. Universal Trauma Syndrome 115

10. Managing The TimeLine 125

11. Reviving HEDONIC Moments 135

12. The Hypnoetics™ Timeline Technique 145

13. Further Advices 155

14. Sensate Awareness 165

15. Signs Of Progress 173

16. Multiple Viewpoint Hypnoetics 181

17. The Complex Of Self 189

18. The Truth About Past Lives 205

19. Re-writing Personal History 215

20. The Protoplasm Entity (PE) 225

21. Better Communication Means Faster Results 237

22. The Undercut 249

23. Where Do I Go From Here? 255

"It IS possible to get out of a trap. However, in order to break out of a prison, one first must confess to being in a prison. The trap is man's emotional structure, his character structure. There is little use in devising systems of thought about the nature of the trap if the only thing to do in order to get out of the trap is to know the trap and to find the exit. Everything else is utterly useless... *The first thing to do is to find the exit out of the trap.*"

- Wilhelm Reich

Punk Psychology™ leads to the exit out of the trap!

PUNK.

Definition: a style or movement characterized by the adoption of outrageously unconventional and often bizarre or shocking clothing, hairstyles, makeup, etc., and the defiance of social norms of behavior, usually associated with punk rock music. (after Dictionary.com)

Hence: far from the midline or accepted norms. Radical. Assertive. Original. Counter-culture.

PREFACE

This book has been a long time in coming but it won't take you long to read. Between these covers you'll find more answers to the workings of the human mind than you ever imagined. Not only that but it's effectively a map: you will be able to *travel* the human mind with it.

A psychonaut!

You will even learn basic skills in fixing and repairing the mind, keeping it fine tuned, developed for best performance, and eradicating issues that lead to unwanted emotions and dysfunctional behaviors.

You can do this! It doesn't take psychologists, counselors, licensed therapists or any other money-grabbing "helpers" with addled ideas. It just takes people of a good heart, a quick wit, and average intelligence, coupled with the amazing Punk Psychology™ techniques explained in this book.

Can you imagine the effect on our world if people just STOPPED being crazy, destructive, vicious, and hysterical? It would be like a dream... no more wars, no more murders, in fact no crime at all! That would mean no more armed police and no more armies needed to fight and kill supposed enemies!

Politicians would become sane and honest; they would govern for the people, not their own gain; government would eventually become what it is supposed to be: a system of effective management that is there to serve the individuals in society and allow them to lead the kind of life they choose! As a result of that, taxes would be something we were all more willing to pay over, since we could see the money being used how we wanted!

Divorce rates would plummet; delinquency would become a thing of the past; popular music could celebrate all the good things in life, instead of whining and moaning about loss and betrayal; mental hospitals would empty out (and a good lot of patients in regular hospitals could go home too, because stress is behind most sickness); animal welfare wouldn't be needed; drugs such as antidepressants and tranquillizers could be consigned to the history books; poverty and misery would fade from the world, as people woke up to the fact that we are all here on the same terms and just grabbing what we want, at the expense of others, would eventually bring the whole world grinding to a halt.

It all starts with the human mind. So the solutions must also start with the human mind. Can we understand ourselves fully and correct what's not working properly? I passionately believe so and have plenty of cases and experience to back up what I say.

There are answers. Real answers. Punk Psychology™ (PP) can do this!

There is far too much mystique out there, disinformation, myth and nonsense, created by under-performing researchers, who insist on confusing the mind with the brain and equate consciousness with perceptions, which are both follies of the first magnitude.

Not only are they scrabbling in the wrong direction, trying to understand the mind. They have the cheek to argue you can't go there! It's their domain of skills, they claim. Ha! We have our very existence based in a mind and you are as entitled as anyone else to learn about yourself, to experiment, to follow threads of reasoning, and to test experience for yourself.

This book will help you travel into the world within and reveal to you some amazing principles. It will also teach you skills that will enable you to swiftly, easily and permanently change bad emotions into good; reckless behaviors into success strategies; and troubling thoughts into torrents of joy and inspiration!

You will quickly come to understand that the mind is neither consciousness, nor perception. It's an interface between consciousness and the material environment. Its primary algorithm (steps of procedure) you will learn later is to orient the organism (you and me) properly in its surroundings. It enables us to be here and function, safely and effectively.

Without the mind's primary algorithm, we would not survive very long. It's that important.

This crucial algorithm is introduced on page 69.

Mind Beyond The Brain

Science is obsessed with what I call brain-based being (B3). That's the untenable notion that all of our awareness, feelings, perceptions, beliefs, decisions and imagination come from brain function and only from brain function.

The joke is, none of the above come from the brain—or even have anything to do with the brain. How can I say that?

Along with millions of people who have travelled outside their body (and think nothing of doing it), I know full well that we don't need eyes to see, we don't need ears to hear, we don't need the body to think. We are just taught to believe that we do. As kids we know better; kids live in a different world, where the mind creates reality; where reality is personal, flexible and exciting.

Things can happen and UN-happen at will!

But eventually that is battered out of us by adults, demanding that we stop fantasizing and learn "how things really are".

So phenomena like remote viewing, out-of-body, telepathy and clairvoyance are scorned and denigrated. They couldn't happen, says mechanistic science, so they don't. It's all a hoax. What about the cases that prove these things really do happen? Well, that's just delusion (or fraud), they say.

The issue is what we call the extended mind. See, science says the mind is in the brain. Truth says the brain is in the mind! All of our experience comes from the mind. But the mind is far greater than the 3-lb blob of jelly inside our skulls.

Here's a simple test to get you started:

Close your eyes and think of a cat (elephant, flower vase, banjo, anything you like). Now picture it clearly in your mind's eye. Before opening your eyes, point to where that picture exists. Like 99% of the human race, you'll likely point to a spot about eight inches in front of your face.

That's where the mental image picture lies... outside the skull. But science says that's only an illusion; it's really inside your skull. *Yet they cannot produce a single shred of evidence to prove that ridiculous claim. Their* only wobbly position is that your mind image "must be" inside the skull. Why? Because the mind is in the brain, they say.

But you've just proved it isn't.

So where does that leave the truth? It's your truth; you just proved it to yourself. Do not let slippery science tell you that you are wrong. As I said, there is NO evidence of any kind that the mind and memory is in the brain.

The brain is simply a tuner, an interface between the mind and so-called reality. It can be likened to a smart phone: using your device you can connect with cities all round the world, talk to friends, call up notes and reminders, just like the mind! Does that mean that your friends, or cities elsewhere in the world, are actually inside your phone? Of course not! No more is your mind in your brain.

The mind is actually non-material. Thoughts are not material, which is why scientists can't properly measure or classify them. They are on the wrong model. The best they can do is suggest certain parts of the brain light up, when you think about women, happiness, your pet dog, or a math puzzle.

Well, you'd expect that, if the brain was nothing more than a tuner. It doesn't prove that the brain is self-aware or capable of thinking.

OK, one more proof and then I'm done... did you know that some people can lose 98% of their brain tissue and yet nobody could tell the difference? Remarkable as it seems, this has happened to some patients suffering from a condition called hydrocephalus. All that remains is a thin 1 or 2 millimeter smear of brain tissue round the inside of the skull.

Yet these people think, feel and act normally, their memory is no worse than the rest of us. One was even an accountant and held down a professional career, without anyone being aware of a problem.

And consider this: we all use the expression "running around like a headless chicken". But did you know a number of chickens have survived for several weeks after having their heads cut off? Providing a human pours food and water down the gullet, these decapitated animals (without any brain at all) can walk around and function almost normally. According to the *UK Daily Mail* (29 March 2018), the chicken that survived longest without its head is believed to be one named Mike, who lived for 18 months after losing his head in Utah (USA) in 1945.

Not that I am saying the brain is worthless. We all know that if the motor areas get damaged, paralysis can result. If the speech areas are compromised, then that individual may be unable to form words.

But that doesn't mean the brain thinks! Only that it is in the pathways of perception, transmission and communication. Back to the smartphone: I am saying that if you damage the microphone, your voice can't be heard by the caller. But it doesn't mean you didn't speak! If you drop the phone and smash the screen, that doesn't mean you vanished! Brain dysfunction does not mean that you can't think. In fact many celebrated cases have reported that when they were supposedly "unconscious" or paralyzed, they were thinking and feeling 100% normally.

Jean-Dominique Bauby dictated a whole book while he was locked within because his brain wouldn't function and connect. The medical name for this unfortunate state is locked-in syndrome. So his mind was present; all body function was largely lost as a result of massive brain damage. We know all this from reading his book, *The Diving Bell and The Butterfly*, which was dictated while blinking an eyelid, they only part of him left that could respond to his thoughts.

There is a journal on my desk at this very moment (*New Scientist*, vol 233, No 3111, 4 Feb 2017, p.11), with an article explaining that electronic devices reveal that locked-in people think like the rest of us. Their brain is largely trashed (at least judged by the total inability to move) and yet they share all our joys, jokes, emotions and desires.

All I am saying is that the brain is not the mind: it does not think, it does not feel; it does not dream. It's the switchboard.

The actual mind is infinite in extent.

Mind As A Field

The idea of an extended mind is not so strange if it really is a field. Fields are all the rage in science these days. The important property of a field is that it is infinite. There are no boundaries. There are no holes in it.

A field stretches out to the ends of the universe (and maybe beyond, who knows?) True, the field weakens as you move further out. We call that *attenuation*. But it only applies to physical fields, such as nuclear attraction forces, magnetism and gravity.

There is nothing to say that non-material fields attenuate. Since science says there are no non-material fields, it is short on opinion about this. But the quantum field or the zero-point field or even space-time as a field have no ends and do not attenuate.

If the mind is a field, it is infinite.

So if the mind is a field, we can make certain predictions. These are our first "punk points":

- It can perceive things far beyond the body
- Telepathy and remote viewing are a given
- Prescience is likely and will occur often
- The past and future of Being are infinite
- Consciousness is immanent in all things
- The past and present of all things are present in all things (the so-called holographic model)
- Knowledge is time and place
- Memory is part of the field and is therefore non-material

I submit that all these predictions are readily provable, once the dogma of materiality is dropped.

Memory Is Not In The Brain

While we are on the topic, memory is not in the brain either. I just remarked that people who lose 98% of their brain cortex do not suffer any memory impairment.

You may read of examples where the human brain was damaged and the person could not recall properly and feel that vindicates the brain as a memory organ theory. It doesn't. If you take your computer and throw away the keyboard and screen (the interface), that means you can't communicate with it properly. You won't be able to get at the memory. But the files are still there! The memory itself is unchanged on the internal drive. Brain damage is really just damage to the keyboard and track pad interface.

The truth is the brain does not—and cannot—do the job that science ascribes to it.

In 1904 a German biologist called Richard Semon (1859 – 1918) wrote what is now a classic book on mind and memory. Its title is *The Mneme* (a word which has since been stolen by Richard Dawkins and others, adapted as the meme or so-called "thought virus").

[*The Mneme* 1904; reprint, London: George, Allen and Unwin, London, 1921]

Sadly, Semon committed suicide shortly after World War One ended, wrapped in a German flag, allegedly because he was depressed by Germany's defeat. But his almost-forgotten work lives on and has a lot to teach us and is now enjoying a considerable revival.

In a nutshell, Semon wrote about memory recording, which he called a process of *engraphy* (literally "writing inwards") and the resulting memory trace was an *engram*. That's another of his words that have been widely adopted in scientific use. Papers continue to be published regarding engrams. The most famous of all time was Karl Lashley's seminal research, culminating in a lasting work: "In Search of the Engram", *Symposia of the Society for Experimental Biology 4* (1950): 454–482.

The belief was that memory is some kind of physical trace in the brain. Semon himself rejected the idea that engrams could be something immaterial or metaphysical (p.275), though he was smart enough to admit that he was associating the phenomena he was writing about with "invisible structures whose existence is a matter of pure imagination" (p. 276).

Lashley cut up the brains of laboratory rats, piece by piece, until there was virtually no brain left—yet still the rats did not suffer any measurable deterioration of memory learning! We can conclude that memory is not physical.

Yet scientists struggle on, trying to prove their theories are correct, instead of searching for the truth. The latest research I found was as recent as 2010 [Josselyn, S.A. (2010). "Continuing the search for the engram: examining the mechanism of fear memories" *Journal of Psychiatry and Neuroscience* 35, p. 221-228].

The Speed Of Memory Is An Anomaly

I found an interesting study (Nov 2015) that makes it clear that memory function (recording and retrieval) is so fast that neurons and synapses in the brain cannot possibly be involved in the process, except maybe peripherally, but certainly not as the causal agency.

Richard Semon was very smart and the first scientist to point out that memory was not simply a matter of recording impressions (the engram). There had to be some kind of retrieval system too, otherwise the memories could not be accessed!

The retrieving of memories Semon named ecphory, or awakening of the previous engramic record.

Here is a synopsis of the study findings:

They conducted two experiments with human participants. In the first, they "encoded" memories with some specific tags they called "retrieval cues" (triggers for remembering).

There was then a memory test with the retrieval cues presented dead center, instead of to the right or left. EEG showed brain activity leapt into life very early (around 100- 200 milliseconds), on one side or the other.

This showed, in the words of the researchers, there was a clear pre-conscious element to memory and it was very fast.

As a refinement, they used rhythmic transcranial magnetic stimulation (electromagnetic waves directly through the skull) to interfere with early memory retrieval processing, stimulating either the right or left brain separately. The result was interference with the memory that had its retrieval cue on the opposite side.

To quote the researchers,

"These results demonstrate, for the first time, that episodic memory functionally relies on very rapid reactivation of sensory information that was present during encoding."

Episodic memory means recall of experiences and events (episodes). The other main type of memory is learning memory, repetition, by which we learn our math tables or how to ride a bicycle.

But what the researchers didn't say, because they weren't looking for it (it landed in their blind spot), is that this is too fast for brain-activated memory!

Transmission within the nervous system across synapses (the gaps between brain cells) is ten times slower than transmission through nerve fibers; typically about 2 milliseconds to cross the gap. The 100-millisecond delay they were finding would allow connection through only 50 – 100 brain cells at most. Hardly enough to record the smell, sound, colors, emotion, words, lighting, body posture and all the other dozens of memory modalities for even a single instant of memory!

They need a new theory! They just virtually "proved" that the brain only processes memories, it does not handle or record them!

We'll be dealing with episodic memory extensively in this text. Hypnoetics™ is all about experiential memory; travelling the timeline; cleaning up the debris and restoring the infinite scope of mind.

Time to get started!

But first let me say just one thing:

I'm talking real knowledge here, not fanciful ideas. I wrote this book personally. I've evolved this method by experiment and testing. It did not come "from God" or a burning bush, or tablets of gold! In other words, you don't have to take anything in faith or on trust! Moreover, it was not "channeled" from some long-dead medieval busybody or translated from the Vedas!

In fact there is a surprising core of science for something that is so new and radical. I invite you to try out what's written on every page of the book. I show you how to do it: you copy the protocols and get a result... then you KNOW it works!

That's a better deal than modern science, where you have to take, entirely on trust, the existence of black holes (nobody has ever seen or touched one), the fact that the Sun is a collapsing star (doesn't fit with the fact that the Sun is hottest in its outer layers!), or that evolution was by pure, random chance (nobody has been around long enough to observe it and the existing evidence doesn't fit that model at all).

By the time you get to about chapter 5 you will realize this is not about meditation, energy psychology so-called, affirmations or "finding the good". This is not anything traditional or familiar. It is an awesome stylish "Tesla" (car), cognitive re-engineering technique that literally re-evaluates and realigns your mental pathways.

Let's call it a soft re-wire. It is truly unique and beyond anything you may have experienced before.

CHAPTER 1

INTRODUCING HYPNOETICS™

The core tool in Punk Psychology® we call Hypnoetics™. Don't be disturbed by the fact that it sounds a bit like hypnotism. Hypnoetics™ is actually UN-hypnotizing people. It's taking them out of their trance, into the NOW!

That might seem a shocking idea—that people are walking around as if asleep. But it's actually not a new concept. French psychiatrist Pierre Janet (1859—1947) actually pioneered many extremely modern advances in the field of the mind. He even invented the term *subconscious mind* and developed amazing techniques that were later grabbed by Freud, who accidentally "forgot" to say he had stolen them from his colleague.

All that's history now and Freud has gone down the tubes, his weird sexual theories almost a historic joke; whereas Janet is literally being re-born, as scientists and psychologists in the 21st century discover his remarkable, insightful work.

Janet wrote about "somnambulism", which you probably know is a medical term that means sleepwalking. The person looks properly tuned in and present; but is not. He or she is not "here" but is working on automatic. And, as the original 19th century pioneers understood, we are all—to a degree—sleepwalking!

We function mostly normally. But we have a significant percentage of our attention units trapped elsewhere. We are in a kind of mind loop, sticking to past unpleasant events. In Supernoetics® we call these unpleasant memories memonemes. The more we have our attention on these issues from the past, the less attention units we have for living in the present. In other words, the more asleep or hypnotized we are!

Influential early 20th-century mystic, philosopher and spiritual teacher, Georges Gurdjieff noticed the problem too. His famous saying was: *the biggest barrier to being conscious (alert and aware) is the delusion that we are already conscious.* Most people are not. Not fully.

Our task in Punk Psychology® then, is to DE-hypnotize people and get them back to the present. It's like sending out the lifeboat, to rescue them from rough seas of the mind, and then bring them safely ashore, to relaxation, calm and insight (awareness).

You can perhaps imagine that by getting our attention off many troublesome events from the past, that we become more alert, brighter, quicker at thinking and with less "baggage" in our emotional processes. In fact that's just how it feels: clean, clear, alert and efficient in mind! A spotless memory!

How do we do this? It's simple (you can learn to do it, as this book will show): we guide or "pilot" the person to wherever he or she is stuck in the past and UN-stick them! We call it GPS for the mind!

Regression: isn't that old fashioned?

Nope. True, the idea has been around a long while (since 1868, when Dutch physician Andries Hoek provided the first case study of cathartic hypnotherapy in fact) but the actual modern technique we use—easy, fun and very effective—was only developed by me and a handful of colleagues in the late 20th century.

We call it piloting because it's essentially like steering. Think of it like a riverboat pilot, knowing what to do and where to go.

So, far from being an old procedure, Punk Psychology® is really a modernization of a well-established (proven) concept.

Without The Electronics

Don't be overawed, however. I am going to show you how you can perform this miracle of recovery, frequently, even routinely, and help your fellow man step out into the light and live a different kind of life, free of the encumbrance of past miseries. The use of a GSR meter is not mandatory, except perhaps for those doing this work professionally.

Most importantly, we do not need drugs or any other chemical "solution" to improve mental function and performance. We are not trying to "solve" a difficulty, or come up with an answer or adaptation. We fully eradicate the dependence on the unpleasant emotions of the past.

Thing is, all negative emotions and unsuccessful behaviors (ineffective strategies, you might say) were installed for a reason. They worked once. But that was then! This is Now! We don't need to go back there every time an issue arises.

Through the true power of the mind, we can create better and forward-thinking moods and behaviors that serve us well. You know the ones from the past don't work! We all aware of that. Yet it can be extremely difficult to stop dramatizing them (dramatizing: living out the past, move for move, thought for thought).

What I found and proved to my own satisfaction, over and over, is that if you find the episode from the past that is tending to dominate your thinking, is generating unwanted feelings and is forcing you into behavior that you don't want, providing you address it fully and with our special immersion approach, it will evaporate... literally.

Memories, as I have already revealed, is NOT a permanent record or scar on the tissues. They have to be recreated whenever we "remember". So when we alter this process, for our own benefit, these uncomfortable memories become evanescent (evanescent: vanishing, short-lived; this word derives from a form of the Latin verb *evanescere*, which means "to evaporate" or "to vanish").

You don't lose these unpleasant memories. But they are bled of all negative emotional charges and destructive, derivative beliefs, so they become just information, or what I call "clean, useful memory".

That's an important point. If you suffer agoraphobia (fear of the outdoors and open spaces) because of having been attacked in a dark alley, we want you to break out of your fear. But we want you to do it rationally, not from avoidance or denial. To recover fully, not just cope. You will develop a future safety strategy for walking alone, based on what you learned. But the life-impairing fear will be gone. You can recall the events of that night, without quailing or switching on your incapacitating flight-or-fight response. So you now have additional information to process. Your memory of events has become helpful, instead of traumatic.

More about this later.

Unconscious Memory

Again we have cause to be grateful to Pierre Janet, because he discovered hidden and untapped memory. In Punk Psychology® we call these buried memories the "stacks", a library term, meaning all the archives stored in the basement and not generally accessible, without special permission from the librarian!

It's difficult to believe, in our day and age, that it was once supposed that if you couldn't remember an event, the memory simply wasn't there. It was vanished. The volume was gone from the shelves in the stacks, if you like. But thanks to Janet's pioneer investigations—given wings and spread through the early part of the 20th century by Freud's plagiarism—we now accept it as a matter of course.

It shows up in movies and TV soaps, for goodness' sake!

Don't underestimate the size and significance of this enormous breakthrough in understanding the mind. If it was really true that what you can't remember cannot disturb you, because it's no longer there, life would be a breeze. But the other model, of unconscious or "subconscious" hurtful memory, is one of Humankind's biggest problems. We are plagued by emotions, nightmares and behaviors caused by events in our past, which we simply cannot remember. They are buried, well and truly.

But they are definitely there. The "librarian" in your mind knows all that stuff is there in the "stacks" and seems unable to refrain from handing out the memory volume, without you being consulted, and often to your great disadvantage. It takes a specific trigger to cause the volume to be opened and released (this is continuing the library metaphor, avoiding complex scientific language). But whenever that trigger comes along in life, the librarian does her stuff and out comes the whole book—and a good few related volumes at times!

You suddenly feel upset, yucky, irritable, get strange pains and sensations or your concentration goes off the rails. Perhaps you started reading the book of lost loves. Suddenly all your lost loves books are out and opened at once, three, five, maybe dozens of stories, come back to stir you up!

Thing is, the librarian is not a dope. In fact she's ruthlessly efficient. She's a whizz at her job. Think about it: if you asked her to recall every occasion on which you wore a particular jacket, she could turn up lots of files; if you asked for holidays at the seaside, she's got all those indexed and cross-indexed too; if you ask her for exciting sex memories, no problem; Italian works of art, sure; embarrassing moments, oh we have LOTS of those!

It's true isn't it that it's easier for her to find tricky or uncomfortable memories than sweet ones that make you sigh with delight. That's not her fault; that's how you lived your life. But Punk Psychology® will change all that too. *Your take on things will improve quickly and comprehensively as you clean out the old stacks and get your memories re-classified as "clean and useful"!*

So You Think You Know?

About to be revealed is the Punk Psychology® number one secret to a new and happy life: *what you think is wrong is not it!* Or put another way, where you think the problem is coming from is never correct.

There is a simple rule: when you find the source of an issue, it vanishes. It's a kind of psychology functional magic we call Deep-IS. The surface layer, the Simple-IS is what appears on the outside; that's how it looks. But it cannot be true because, if it was, the problem would vanish in a puff. Deep-IS is a special kind of impermanence; it's the same magic at the moment of creation as at the moment of vanishment.

Zen philosophy and many sages over the ages have noticed that truth is ephemeral... Time (persistence) is a lie and only attained by altering something; in other words making it less than true. Anything which persists contains falseness. Real truth evaporates, to become part of the infinite field of all-knowing.

Of course this is the opposite of what people suppose. *Real truth is eternal and never changes.* It's a world-class hoax (faulty idea which "everybody knows" is true, like the earth is flat!) However, the commonly held view is w-r-o-n-g! That's why humans have never been able to spring the trap that holds them fast.

Does this sound troubling and complex? Don't worry. It may be, at first sight. But you will work with this axiomatic truth throughout this book and discover for yourself that real truth does not contain persistence. Hence the difficulties we encounter only persist because there is a lie. Once you get past the lie, to the real buried truth (Deep-IS), the problem simply disappears. That's great.

We have a technical expression for this: *negative gains.* Getting good results by dropping out what is not wanted. No, it's not a joke. It's a very real mechanism. When you find the real reason for an effect, the deeper truth, is vanishes like morning mist in the noonday sun!

Case Example: I had a client, a lady in her thirties, who was afraid of cats. She "knew" why she was afraid of cats, she told me. At the age of four years she had been attacked by a mean tomcat, which bit her and badly scratched her.

I took her back down the timeline, using the PP immersion method I will describe later in this book, and I quickly found she was w-r-o-n-g! The real (true) reason for her fear of cats was a memory we uncovered from the age of just a few months.

Her mother had put her in a crib and set it out in the sunshine in the yard, so that the infant may have some fresh air, while Mom did her chores. Unfortunately, a wily cat slipped into the nice warm spot in the crib and went to sleep on the baby's face.

When mother discovered this she yelled in anguish, "*The baby is dead! The cat has killed the baby. My baby has suffocated. She cannot breathe. The evil cat has killed my little child...*" on and on, as mothers might, given the situation.

But the child was not dead and easily able to breathe under the fluffy cat. Now bear in mind that an infant of just a few months has no language. She didn't understand the words. But she did get the fear and grief emanating from her mother. It was very stressful.

The force rolled up in the memory was what made her afraid of cats, once it was triggered by the later event of being scratched and bitten. How do I know for sure? The woman howled with laughter for a full half hour and was never afterwards afraid of cats. In fact she giggled every time she saw one and even stroked them freely.

So Do We All End Up As Identical Plastic Dolls?

Not on my watch! The truth is, by shedding unwanted strife and negativity, we come in time to be more our own unique selves, not more like everybody else.

The actuality seems to be that the dark mechanisms of the mind are somewhat universal in character and effect. We share those. The light, free, good-humored personal aspect of our thoughts and character is the part that is unique to us.

So don't worry; we are talking personal freedom and expanded awareness, not cookie-cutter mentality!

But without your pain and emotions, aren't you a poor shadow of a human being? That's a common misconception you will certainly come across. Again, it's misguided. Yes, stormy emotions, ridiculous beliefs and absurd destructive behaviors are common, even as you might say normal, but that doesn't make the poor functioning state most people are in something desirable.

C'mon! Road rage doesn't make you a better driver, now does it?

The idea that it is noble to suffer and we need emotional hurt and strife is, quite frankly, baloney. In Punk Psychology® we call these "everybody knows it's true" follies a hoax. Hoaxing is a widespread vice we'd like to get rid of! Especially this one: that behaving badly and throwing our negative emotions all over the place is not just desirable; it's our right or entitlement!

What complete and insupportable nonsense. It's peddled largely by people who cannot cope with their irrationality and emotional overload. Getting drunk continuously or taking mind-invasive drugs is not needed to be a creative and productive person.

Ask Michelangelo! He didn't need self abuse to create his masterpieces, though it is generally accepted that he had some kind of *terribilitá* (Italian word for driven by personal demons of overwhelming intensity)

Physical Health ···

Now, earlier, I hinted that unpleasant physical sensations, such as aches and pains, nausea, headache or fatigue, can come from charged events deep within the mind.

This is so.

You have probably heard the term psychosomatic, which means "in the body, coming from the mind". It's often used pejoratively; the idea being that people who suffer from psychosomatic ills are somehow inadequate or weak-minded.

This is a foolish notion. Take pain. The idea that there is "real" pain and imaginary pain—pain from peripheral pain nerves or pain only from within the mind—doesn't stand up. *All pain is processed at brain level and experienced in the mind, not in the nerves or tissues.* That's why we can anesthetize someone by shutting down mind function temporarily.

The doctors express this as saying that pain is a central phenomenon.

OK, with that out of the way, let's move to the important point here, which is that stress and mental trauma are strenuously visited on the body. This is not a slight thing. I'm not just talking aches and pains, rashes or bellyaches; I'm talking heart disease, crippling arthritis, autoimmune disease, cancer and even the possibility of death. Even the way genes express themselves is proven to be influenced by our thoughts. Anything that can go wrong with the body can get started with trouble in the mind.

Medicos in the know have a rule: if a person gets sick, *stress or psychic trauma leading up to that sickness is always a factor.* Stress causes illness. This can be as simple as a cold or sore throat, which often follows loss or sudden shock. Or it can be as severe as cancer coming on after the departure of a loved one (death or divorce).

We'll talk about it more in a subsequent chapter. For now, just keep this clearly in your head: the mind powerfully impacts bodily health and disease, as surely as bodily damage and ills can influence the way we feel in mind. Put in simpler words, the mind influences biology as surely as biology influences the mind.

There's a great book I will be introducing in later pages by Harvard professor Bessel van der Kolk, called *The Body Keeps The Score*. This phenomenon is big in Punk Psychology®.

It's called *somatization*, from the Greek word soma, meaning body. It has nothing to do with malingering or faking symptoms for financial or other reward. It has everything to do with the fact that our total experience of the world begins and ends with the mind and a mind in turmoil will, sooner or later, result in physical symptoms in the body!

Helping Others ·······································

The great thing about Punk Psychology® is that you can use it to help people around you, all the time! You can also buddy up with someone and hack away at each other's lousy emotions and irrationality. That's why it's optimistic punk!

Some of us feel (or believe) we are leading very good, meaningful lives. Maybe we are not struggling, as so many people are, to find happiness, purpose and reward in life.

That doesn't mean we have no interest in the mechanics of mind and the structures of a workable philosophy of success. It just means we need to develop the expertise of helping others who are not so fortunate and may be making heavy weather of it all.

The thing is, how could it not be valuable and life-changing to get a grasp of some of the key mechanics of the mind and its workings?

You could become the go-to person for your tribe or network. It really is electrifying to be able to recognize what someone is experiencing and know why it is happening to them. As you share your knowledge, people will look to you for solutions and advice.

Remember, the mother of Punk Psychology® (called Supernoetics®) is itself a body of knowledge with a HUGE library of protocols, workshops, tips and rubrics that can solve just about any life situation. Punk Psychology® is only a small part of the whole; but a very handy part, nonetheless.

CHAPTER 2

With Punk Psychology® you will be able to raise "Real IQ". What is that? Why is it different from academic IQ, the one normally measured by IQ tests?

It is a common observation, almost an axiom (self-evident truth), that most of us are operating at far less than our full mental and physical potential. Nobody knows just what the human mind is capable of, though we have been given a number of tantalizing glimpses by a few outstanding individuals:

For example young Mozart is said to have astounded contemporaries by writing out the entire score of Allegri's Miserere from memory, after only one hearing.

Shakuntala Devi, a lady from Calcutta, worked out the twenty third root of a 201 digit number in just fifty seconds (it took a computer a full minute to confirm that she was right but it needed over 13,000 instructions beforehand).

In 1960 in San Francisco George Koltanowski played 56 consecutive unbeaten games of blindfold chess (without sight of the board), at an average speed of 10 seconds per move. He beat 50 opponents and drew with 6, all able to see the board and pieces.

In 1967 Mehmed Ali Halici, from Turkey, recited from memory all 6,666 verses of the Koran in six hours, word perfect.

Kim Ung-Yong of Seoul, at the age of 4 years 8 months, wrote poetry, spoke four languages and was adept at integral calculus.

You've probably heard of those brilliant youngsters called savants, sometimes brain injured (autism, etc.), who have AMAZING powers of mind. Savant Stephen Wiltshire has been nicknamed "The Human Camera": he has taken one helicopter ride over Rome and drawn the entire city from memory, every building, rooftop and all the windows where they should be. It's almost incomprehensible.

Compared to these spectacular achievements, the mental power that most of us can muster is on the order of a wet firecracker to a nuclear bomb. The question however is not "How do they do it?" but "Why can't we do things like that?" "Is there something wrong with the rest of us?"

No. In fact we are simply distracted; we have our attention units stuck in the past. We are, if you like, hypnotized by our past. It lives with us in the present. To be more efficient in the NOW, we have to recover our attention units from where they are held in time!

It's a simple enough concept. Indeed it's very simple to do, once you have the technique I am going to teach you here.

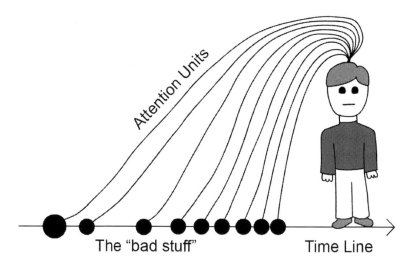

Attention Units

The "bad stuff"   Time Line

The thing is, once you start recovering your attention units into the NOW, you can start to solve life's problems far more easily. It's memory confusion and hidden memory override of facts that makes us irrational. We have more of what in Punk Psychology® we call "clear mind space"; that's the part of the mind that functions optimally. It's the opposite of the reductionist, foolish thinking that we so often get into.

More clear mind space means more of what I call "adaptive intelligence", which is the amount of reasoning power and intelligence a person has with which to solve real problems in life, not the picture puzzles and "missing numbers" that they throw at you in an academic IQ test.

Not that I am suggesting everyone is a latent genius and simply by following my methods outlined here you will automatically become one. But what I am saying is that by using Punk Psychology® to understand the fundamental reasons that our mental powers are under-used—and getting rid of the worst of these encumbrances—anyone can raise his or her abilities to as-yet-undreamed-of levels.

You must do this, if you are to achieve the success you are looking for, whether it is fame, fortune, romantic love or just happiness and immortality.

Seeking Happiness •••

Unfortunately, the failure to live up to our potential seems to hold true not just considering objective parameters such as "intelligence" and reaction time but also vague subjective criteria, like happiness, health and success.

I have yet to meet a person who didn't think there were many times in life when they could have done things differently and been happier for it. Failure is a universal experience at some time or other. We even have a saying, "It is human to err", as if getting it right and succeeding all the way down the line is somehow inhuman and not quite nice!

Of course there are times when we each of us feels wonderfully happy and content. At such moments of bliss we wouldn't change places with anyone else in the world. But if we are honest, such occasions are few and far between and seem to happen only by serendipity. It is rather like being tossed about in a turbulent sea of misfortune on a small raft and having no means of steerage. Islands are the times of joy and it is pure luck whenever we make a successful landfall.

Often, as the years advance, land is seen less and less often until finally the ocean seems empty and we are doomed to drift on it until one final storm sends us to the bottom.

But we can change that! Punk Psychology® to the rescue!

Irrational Behavior

Why do we do things we shouldn't? As a species it is remarkable that we have been so successful because it seems at times that we are driven by a relentless madness which urges us into actions which are not only irrational but highly destructive, both to ourselves and others. The fact that it is a universal experience makes such behavior no less incomprehensible, yet by the very mystery of its origins we feel helpless to prevent it. And so, in the aftermath of our folly, all we can do is sigh with regret and count the cost.

How often do you hear the expression "I don't know what came over me"? That is exactly the way it happens; something seems to gain control, a different YOU, and while it has the upper hand we are forced to act out of character. You hear this in the pathetic excuses made by mass murderers, embezzlers, rapists and other villains.

But it applies equally well to the lesser mistakes and misdemeanors of everyday people like you and me, acts that might be described as unkind, confused, foolish, hurtful, embarrassing or just plain nasty. You can probably think of hundreds of examples, major and minor, of the kind of human weakness I am talking about. Yet these are not typical or wished-for behaviors of the perpetrator. Far from it.

These acts seem to come from deep within, from a part of the mind that skulks away in the darkness and remains resolutely out of view.

If doing things that are nuts were not enough, then comes the maddening frustration of not acting when we ought to. More than all the times we have hurt or been hurt are those moments when life presented us with a golden opportunity which—through neglect, fear, folly or other failing—somehow passed us by and so the fame, glamor, riches or success that we craved so earnestly still evaded us.

The hard-working clerk who is passed over for promotion; the sweet girl who gets the wrong man in marriage and ends up a battered wife; the child whose musical talent is stifled and dies; the would-be writer who somehow never sells a line of his work; the rich man who drinks excessively and dies all too young; the promising actor who will not moderate his sexual proclivities and contracts fatal hepatitis... these and many other human stories are played out each day.

It seems as if the common condition for human life here on earth is that we suffer and fail. In the words of fellow-physician and philosopher Oliver Wendell Holmes:

"Too many people die with their music still in them. Why is it so? Too often it is because they are always getting ready to live. Before they know it, time has run out."

Emotions ··

Isn't the real problem our inappropriate destructive emotions and the force they exert over us? Negative emotions, it is true, are generally accompanied by irrationality. I don't think emotions are the origin of the foolishness—rather that both come from the same cause: buried experiences that we call *memonemes*, about which you'll learn later [just don't forget our emotions can also be powerfully motivating forces. We wouldn't have much incentive to act without excitement, anticipation or pleasure. Even anger and fear will get us off our ass and into real-time].

It seems it isn't enough to be cursed with ridiculous and destructive actions that bring about failure, we are also forced to submit to unpleasant and inappropriate feelings, which make it seem worse. A pop singer, whose records sold more than any other individual up to that time, is fabulously rich, adored by millions and wants for nothing; yet he is miserable and lonely and poisons himself with drugs every day and eventually dies tragically young. An abbot, highly respected, even revered, a wonderful teacher and in every way someone to look up to, suddenly gives in to homosexual desires, runs away with his lover man and is disgraced. A composer, who scored some of the most sublime music ever penned by man, cannot stand Jews and regards them as less than human. One of the richest men of his era, friend of the stars, lives a wretched and isolated life because of fear. Not fear of being gunned down or even fear of social encounters but fear of germs. He is obsessed with cleanliness and cannot face the idea of contact with anything unclean, including doorknobs or anything touched by other humans.

But if you think these examples imply that what I am saying isn't applicable on a wider scale, or has no relevance in connection with lesser lives, then think of the times you were unhappy when others around you were glad, angry when there was no just cause and your bad temper hurt another, afraid when there was no cause for alarm or you felt hatred, disgust or loathing for someone who had done you no ill and you had no justification for such unbecoming attitudes.

If the reader is like the rest of us he or she will have had such inappropriate thoughts many, many times and it will be a source of hurt and embarrassment to have felt that way at all, never mind frequently.

And like the rest of us, you will probably also be completely baffled as to where these unpleasant feelings and attitudes come from. If you are, rest easy. The answers are known, though not widely enough. My researches for Punk Psychology® have revealed almost everything you would want to knows on this topic. Hey, I'm even going to show you how to deal with some of this; at least the elementary stuff. You may want help from a professional Supernoetics® pilot (quality-of-life coach) at some stage but you and a bunch of caring buddies can do so much for each other too.

That's what this book is about.

Recapturing Attention Units •••••••••••••••••••••••••••••••••••••••

I have already said that Punk Psychology® (Hypnoetics™) is really about UN-hypnotizing people from the past in which they are stuck. In doing so, we recover attention units and our adaptive intelligence soars.

Of course, sheer mental prowess is not a guarantee of success and happiness. The incompetent but brainy professor exists so firmly in reality that he has become the archetype of much humor. No-one needs to be able to work out the 23rd root of a 201 digit number to get ahead at work, pass exams, marry the right girl, enjoy good health and set out on a journey to fulfill one's innermost dream.

A great many ordinary, contented people, without any special skills or attributes, lead wonderful and productive lives and yet they are not among the wealthy or famous. You can tell them because they feel good to be with and one can say with gratitude that, because of such individuals, the world is a better place to live in and happiness is rightly theirs in abundance.

Unfortunately however, not many people can categorize themselves as truly happy. But unless we can discover some way to raise our abilities, success will always elude us and we shall be left feeling unfulfilled and miserable.

Fortunately, it doesn't have to be like that, as we will see...

Adaptive Intelligence

I find what I call "adaptive (functional) intelligence" a better concept than academic intelligence. This adaptive intelligence or knowing has nothing to do with IQ or school performance but simply the person's aptitude in solving problems relating to his or her life and circumstances. I have christened it "Real IQ"!

In fact academic training can be a downright barrier to adaptive knowing; a red herring. It is a cliché, but a valid one, that a university graduate often cannot perform even simple procedures in his specialty without first relearning "from life", to the amusement of uneducated work colleagues, without diplomas, who often have a far better grasp of the fundamentals of their subject.

My own dear father was a farm laborer which, if wages were a measure of man's worth, was a very lowly profession indeed just after the Second World War. Yet he and his colleagues demonstrated a remarkable depth of adaptive intelligence, competence and skills in relation to their work which would make the sophisticated city-dweller seem a half-educated dullard in comparison.

These simple country men had a wide range of skills and learning and had to be, amongst other things, botanists, meteorologists, nutritionists, carpenters, blacksmiths, engineers, drivers, veterinarians, economists, animal keepers, slaughterers, builders and if all else failed... inventors! That they would have performed badly on a test of intelligence to me is more of a comment on the failure of IQ tests than the lack of ability of these farm hands.

Adaptive intelligence, as you will quickly see, is what got us down from the trees, building cars, computers, cell phones and rocket ships... not academic learning. It is powerful, whereas academic knowledge with its diplomas is largely self-reflexive (turned in on itself), in its own little world of books and papers.

Unfortunately, there is no way to measure "adaptive knowing" (functional intelligence) of this kind. The only criterion by which it can be judged is success in the chosen field, and ultimately therefore, happiness and wellbeing. It is worth repeating that successful people come from all walks of life, not just the wealthy.

What we are talking about here is setting a worthwhile goal and being able to overcome all obstacles in the way to achieving it; any self-set goal, any obstacles, any context.

Now that is real intelligence! I would say that true intelligence is the ability to pose and solve problems related to life and circumstances.

And that sums up neatly the primary function of the mind.

There Is A Solution

We can achieve this. We just have to unglue ourselves from the sticky parts of memory and our adaptive IQ soars! We have more clear mind space to reason with. Outcomes leap ahead in quality and desirability. We start getting more of what we want and less of what we don't want!

Take a look at this little figure; you'll see (could be she) has a lot of dark, messy memory clutter. In other words, he's pretty normal!

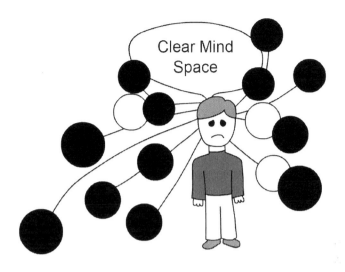

But what if we could get his attention off those dark spots; bring them back to the now? Wouldn't that look better?

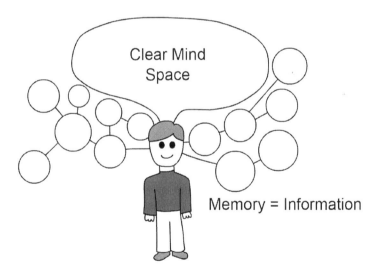

The trick is to pour truth onto what happened in the past. You'll learn to do this with what we call "piloting", that is steering or guiding (like the riverboat pilots of old). As soon as the real story emerges, it tends to vanish in a poof!

But I can remember exactly what happened to me, you say. Well, no. There is always some element of untruth in deep dark memories that are not being fully confronted. The hidden part, that eludes you, that's where the trouble lies.

Read again the account of the lady who was scared of cats (page XXX) and you'll see it in a different light. She remembered being frightened of cats when she was four years old but she did not have access to the earlier memory that really underpinned her fear, until she got expert piloting and went deep-diving into the memory stacks.

Sometimes we even find pre-birth memories or what seem to be earlier incarnations. So there is always the potential of something buried deeply and unknown. See, unknownness is the problem. What we truly know is just information. But if memory is loaded with trauma and can't be accessed easily, it can hurt us without our knowing what's happening. Back to what I said earlier in this chapter about daft behavior and miserable emotions!

Unknownness

You see people doing crazy things. The drunk who is killing himself; the bishop who runs off with a woman in his congregation; the rich earl's son who takes cocaine; or the school teacher who touches up little girls; what lies behind these irrational and self-destructive behaviors?

The person lacks knowledge. They don't know why they do what they do, that much is clear. Otherwise they wouldn't do it (it is accepted that once in a while a bishop would be better to resign and get married, rather than live his life as a hypocrite).

An alcoholic will argue he knows why he drinks. But he goes on killing himself anyway! There is still something unknown in his situation. There is some level below his immediate awareness where the 'solution' of drink was formulated. If he knew what this was, the chances are he would re-visit it and evolve a better way of dealing with the pain of the problem.

This is not a section on alcoholism; drinking to oblivion is merely an example. This rule applies to any and all levels of irrational, purposeless and destructive behavior. You could elevate it to an axiom (self-evident truth): whenever a person is doing badly in life—failing, sick, not prospering, or in any way not standing exactly where he or she wants to be—there is one or more unknown factors in the equation.

Finding and clearing the unknown-ness, as in piloting, brings about an immediate change for the good; there is healing, resolution, improvement, a resurgence of love and energy. The joke is we can know anything we want—we seem to choose to un-know certain things, to hide or bury them, and then proceed to suffer noisily. We pretend to ourselves we don't have the answers we need.

How can I say something so provocative and apparently careless of the suffering of others?

It's simple: after more than four decades of research into mind, emotions and behavior, I can tell you something categorically that is both shocking and yet comical...

Whenever the healing truth finally emerges, it is always something from inside the person.

He or she knew it all along anyway!

There are no outside answers. All the truth we will ever find lies within ourselves. These are words from the great Buddhist scripture the *Dhammapada*, yet they are as true today in the context of modern psychology as they were then, in the wiser days of old.

CHAPTER 3

THE SCALE OF EMOTIONAL AND SOCIAL HEALTH

Here is yet another way of judging adaptive IQ. How does the person get along with others? What are his moods, intentions, purposes and activities around others? It can be very revealing to observe how a person behaves. It will reveal a great deal about his or her "Real IQ".

The following description of this Scale Of Emotional And Social Health is a rudimentary overview and exposure, created by our friend, Jon Whale (UK). I know it will serve as a most useful map.

It is based on the Supernoetics® *Emotional Ladder* but this quick short hand is a great way to be introduced to this very important concept. Emotions are crucial to our lives and thinking. Emotions are a kind of marker; a way of thinking about things. Once an emotional response is attached to a particular person or concept and gets settled onto the body-mind system, these emotional reactions seem to work all on their own.

Often we don't know why a particular emotion arises within us. That makes emotions tricky to manage and, in fact, quite damaging and dangerous. It means we do dumb things and that, in turn, lowers our adaptive IQ.

Individuals who inhabit the upper positive levels of emotional health can employ or drop into any level including the negative levels if required to do so. They will only stay there just as long as they need to achieve a solution. The negative levels can be chronic, i.e. long-standing. Anyone who habituates to any of them may find it arduous to find authentic help or techniques to rise to the higher, positive levels. They are often trapped in the chronic negative levels for the duration of their life.

Nevertheless, using this map, many of you will be able to pinpoint your location and that of family, friends and acquaintances. Read it carefully and try to decide where you are, mostly, and where certain of your friends and family sit!

It starts at the bottom, with the lowest level of emotional and social health, shown here overleaf to the far left at -5 (apathy, despondency, misery, etc.) and goes all the way to +5 on the right (serenity, composure, confidence, etc.) The main characteristics of a person at each level are listed.

Thing is, the rating on this scale correlates very well with Adaptive Intelligence (Real IQ), which is written about elsewhere. The point is that the more charge off your case, the more memonemes are shorn of unknowns and blackness—in other words the more information you have access to—the better your behaviors, interrelationships with others, and the more social and aligned you become.

Rising higher and higher on this scale of social health means more and more adaptive IQ. Below follows a description of the mood, intentions and behaviors of individuals at each level, rising from the worst (Negative minus 5) to the very top (Positive plus 5).

It also heralds growth in the willingness to accept other people as they are, and not challenge, attack, try to reform or reject them. You'll get along far better with other people, in other words!

Supernoetics®

The Scale of Social and Emotional Health

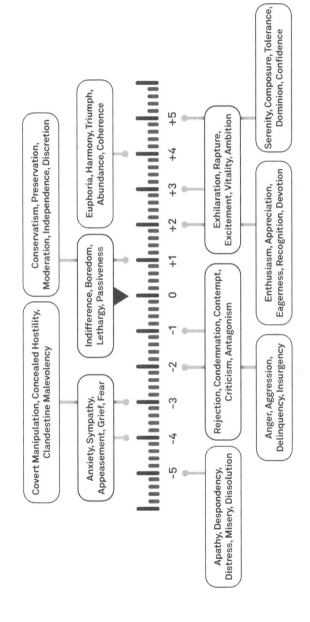

Covert Manipulation, Concealed Hostility, Clandestine Malevolency

Conservatism, Preservation, Moderation, Independence, Discretion

Euphoria, Harmony, Triumph, Abundance, Coherence

Anxiety, Sympathy, Appeasement, Grief, Fear

Indifference, Boredom, Lethargy, Passiveness

Apathy, Despondency, Distress, Misery, Dissolution

Rejection, Condemnation, Contempt, Criticism, Antagonism

Anger, Aggression, Delinquency, Insurgency

Enthusiasm, Appreciation, Eagerness, Recognition, Devotion

Exhilaration, Rapture, Excitement, Vitality, Ambition

Serenity, Composure, Tolerance, Dominion, Confidence

-5   -4   -3   -2   -1   0   +1   +2   +3   +4   +5

Created for Supernoetics® by Jon Whale, Seaton, Devon, UK. Copyright © 2015

Negative Minus 5.
Apathy, Despondency, Distress, Misery, Dissolution

This is the lowest level of Emotional and Social Health.

All emotions are turned off or chemically attenuated.

The core of antisocial behavior.

Many are drug addicts, alcoholics, compulsive gamblers, suicidal psychotics, vagrants, petty drug dealers and lawbreakers, failures, bankrupts, social dependents, institutionalized inmates, the minimalist, or apathetic intellectuals.

They see no point in owning anything, run up debts, which are seldom paid

Allow property and possessions to decay.

Feel helpless and unable to care for themselves.

Slowly self-destruct, bringing down everyone around them.

Rely on handouts and charity.

Never improve, keep making the same mistakes.

Are often actively supported and subsidized by individuals lower on the scale at Negative Minus 4.

They are fed up with life, the world and society, which are to them superficial and no longer interesting.

Negative Minus 4.
Anxiety, Sympathy, Appeasement, Grief, Fear

In deep fear.

Here individuals and groups smother creativity and enthusiasm by using pseudo-kindness, leniency, sympathy and generosity.

This creates, and fosters in others, the lowest negative

They collect and help losers, the sick, down and outs or good causes for the purpose of using them to demonstrate their merciful and compassionate generosity and good intentions.

These self-righteous strategies are used to induce feelings of guilt and shame in people of higher positive emotional levels.

They have an overwhelming fear of hurting others and they never turn their back on anyone they deem is in need.

They provide infinite justifications for failure, they presume nobody is all bad and always give the benefit of the doubt.

Pampering everyone, waiting on them, doing favors for them, refusing to accept anything in return, they prevent unfortunate individuals from regaining self reliance, self worth and dignity.

Their children are treated in exactly the same way. This results in those children wanting continual sympathetic attention and so they are always crying, screaming, fighting, or throwing tantrums to get it, never learning to entertain nor educate themselves.

They cling to sentimentality, grief and pain to protect themselves and attract pity, sympathy and empathy.

They constantly worry about health, accidents, crime and disasters.

Paranoid and suspicious, nearly everything is threatening: germs, disease and criminals are just around every corner waiting to strike.

So they never take chances and are too careful as they never know what might happen.

Life has treated them terribly, they whine, are melancholic, dwell in the past, feel betrayed.

Everything is painful. No money, no job and nobody loves them.

They are afraid of hurting others and are caught in indecision.

Show blind loyalty and compulsive agreement.

Negative Minus 3.
Covert Manipulation, Concealed Hostility,
Hidden Malevolency, Sneaky, Sly

This is probably the most populated chronic emotional level in these turbulent times.

Problem: difficult to immediately assess that they are in this category; only time reveals this to individuals higher on the scale as their game strategy unfolds.

Those in chronic grief and apathy (Negative Minus 3 and 4), never comprehend their strategies.

Always present a cheerful facade, often with a nervous laugh and constant smile.

Appear calm, pleasant and resourceful.

Seem to be sympathetically or morally concerned in politely asking probing personal questions about you, your work, your relationships, your sex life, your politics or your religion.

Their anger remains invisible, yet they are petrified of anyone in anger.

Jealous and extremely dangerous.

Cruel cowards.

Manipulative, they engage in gossip readily but have no qualm in covertly twisting facts around, to knife into the back whenever, wherever and to whomever they can.

When confronted, they change the subject to move away from the point and are always rewriting history or changing the truth about past events to suit their current position. They will do and say anything to avoid exposure.

Through their appearance, words, propaganda or advertising they present themselves, their services or products as being 'so nice, so charming, so condescending and so helpful'.

For objectives that they are too lazy or fearful to undertake themselves, they covertly manipulate and subjugate individuals above and below them on the scale to do their bidding and dirty work.

Their targets are any individual, families, tribes, companies or nations that they consider high on the scale and therefore a threat (e.g. +3s, +4s etc.), attempting to bring them down to chronic appeasement, grief and apathy (Minus 4 and Minus 5)

They have little time for children unless they can use them as an introduction or a weapon for manipulation towards their strategy of introverting others down to Negative Minus 3 and Minus 4. They would like everyone on the planet at this level, so they can feel power.

Their unstated aim is to cause ruin, discredit achievements and split up relationships.

At this they can be very successful and gloat when their victims go down into the lower chronic levels of Negative Minus 4 and 5.

Males at this level subconsciously know their fearful limitations. They can be slothful, but have a need to control and suppress women down to the -4 and -5 levels so that they can feel secure in their sexuality, (as also happens in males at -1 and -2).

Males at this level occupying influential or powerful offices can instigate acts of terrorism and war.

You could never trust anyone at this level with your health, your money, your reputation, your safety, your husband, your wife, your children, your business, your company, your country, or this planet.

Negative Minus 2.
Anger, Aggression, Delinquency, Insurgency

Individuals at this chronic level are consumed with animosity towards others and are furious.

They dominate and intimidate others into submission and obedience.

They blame everyone else for their problems.

They collect grudges to justify their anger and dump them on anyone or anything that passes their way.

They destroy property, social conveniences and lives.

Everyone they meet is wrong or obstructing their ambitions.

Expressing no kindness, no consideration, being blatantly dishonest and disloyal, they lie, use intimidation and ambiguity to destroy creativity and satisfaction

They cause sabotage by deliberately instigating situations or circumstances where others will fail; afterwards they accept no blame, excuse or explanation.

They handle children by tyranny, sometimes with brutal punishment to force them, by means of pain, into what they want.

Not being interested in any viewpoints unless it reinforces their position, they do not listen and continually interrupt others' discussions.

Negative Minus 1.
Rejection, Condemnation, Contempt,
Criticism, Antagonism

Interacting with a person that habituates this level can be amusing for a short time, any longer and it can become boring or enraging.

They enjoy, even laugh at, the misfortune of others and never play for the pleasure.

They want to dominate every activity involving others.

Being resentful and mocking, their subsistence depends on finding and engaging a contestant.

Children are there for them to torment and provoke.

They are insensitive, undiplomatic and unsporting.

They love to argue and dispute everything and get a kick out of reducing others to acute anger and lower.

They never listen, continually interrupt, never permitting the other person to establish their point.

They twist facts to defend and satisfy their own reality, doing their utmost to sabotage the position of others.

they do not listen and continually interrupt others' discussions.

Neutral 0.0
Indifference, Boredom, Ambivalence,
Lethargy, Passiveness

They are observers being indifferent, mildly pleasant, inoffensive, purposeless and unconcerned about any issue.

Everything is too much trouble.

With poor concentration and no ambition, they never achieve any outstanding feat.

Not having any purpose, being lazy and careless, neither content nor discontent, they are not particularly helpful and never intimidating.

Like all of the lower negative levels, they want more affluence but cannot consent to own much.

Largely unnoticed, they amble along stuck at some routine job never upsetting anyone and are accepted by most people.

Positive Plus 1.
Conservatism, Preservation, Moderation, Discretion

The conformist, reticent individual who considers everything with careful deliberation.

They demand proof before believing or acting.

They invariably take the soft, safe option to maintain contentment and rely on the authorities to protect them and do their prosecuting.

They resist change and discourage exploration and innovation.

They are not very tolerant of others in the chronic negative levels, insisting that laws should be made to contain them.

Positive Plus 2.
Enthusiasm, Appreciation, Eagerness, Recognition, Devotion

The genuinely helpful and constructive active person with good personal conviction.

They have a quiet sense of wellbeing and look forward to the day's activities and work.

They can express a wide range of emotions when called for.

Although not yet a leader, not wanting to take sides, they are active people who inspire others to action.

Are always willing to accept more responsibility towards a larger horizon.

They like a good standard of living.

They can spend time with the low emotional levels of people without getting depressed, compulsively sympathetic or exhausted.

Positive Plus 3.
Exhilaration, Rapture, Excitement, Vitality, Ambition

Charismatic personality.

Attract people without effort.

Loved by almost everyone.

Can maintain a strong, sustained interest in their subjects.

Preoccupied with involvement and creativity, they never start something and give in easily.

They are not grasping nor greedy, but are not afraid of possessions.

Not able to tolerate gossip or defamation.

They expect honest facts and, if not forthcoming, they cease communication.

They dislike generalities, insinuations and assumptions.

Have broad spectrum and novel interests.

They can conceive influential plans and ideas that thrust toward a better future for themselves and others.

For them making a fortune is easy and can normally embrace abundant ambitions for survival.

Positive Plus 4.
Power, Harmony, Triumph, Abundance, Coherence

These individuals believe and respect the rights of others.

Honesty, affection, ethics, trustworthy, diplomatic, confidential, discrete, discriminating, communicative, are some of the credits of this level.

They do not interfere with or damage others' lives, business or personal affairs, being more concerned about the survival and future of society and the environment.

Always striving for higher standards for people at lower levels on the scale, they listen to others and understand them easily and can help low level people upwards, without being critical or derogatory.

Enjoying and encouraging children to express themselves, they care for their mental and physical well being.

Positive Plus 5.
Sublime Radiance, Composure,
Tolerance, Puissance, Confidence

This is the highest emotional level.

The benevolent hero and champion.

Individuals at this level are rare and priceless.

They can look at new ideas, change viewpoints, being intuitively spontaneous, light-hearted and humorous.

Neither modest nor egotistical, avoiding snooping and investigation.

They know their abilities and what they are worth.

They like themselves and do not care what others think.

They can follow orders but under no circumstances will they compromise their ethics, but if forced to do so will fight with determination.

Should they decide to do something it will be done and should anyone try to stop them, they do so at their own peril. Plus 5s possess tremendous personal power (puissance) to calm worried or troubled people and find resolutions to the world's problems.

They never hold grudges and stay on good terms with most people by reserving a magnanimous and light-hearted nature.

They excel, without having to control or dominate people to satisfy their own ego.

Their enthusiasm and confidence inspires others to reach higher levels and do things for themselves.

Using The Scale of Emotional and Social Health

Here's a Useful Working Hack

It is a simple matter to integrate the eleven emotional levels of health into your life. Make a list of people that you have known or know well. They can be relations, neighbors, colleagues, politicians, prime ministers, presidents, historical characters, TV and other media personalities, news reporters and commentators; in fact anyone that you know, living or dead. For example, many television soap operas comprise characters acting in the chronic low levels of emotional health on the scale; while the script writers of situation comedies often use characters acting in the higher levels of emotional health.

When you have made the list, compare each person's behavior to the eleven levels of emotional health to determine their chronic or long-standing emotional level.

Jon Whale tells me when he first tried this exercise, he made a list of all of the people past and present who directly and indirectly participated or affected his life. It was very disheartening to discover that over seventy percent of those on his list were categorized in the chronic negative levels.

You may find the same thing. It is a rare to find anyone who has not been exposed to Punk Psychology® much higher than 'chronic conservatism' on this scale (Plus 1). The reason for many a person's melancholy is due to a belief which forms, that people high on the scale of emotional health are in short supply, while those low on the scale seem to be very common.

However, you will be disappointed to discover that love and peace is not the solution. Extending these sentiments, showing others the 'pink light' only provides an invitation for individuals low on the scale, (-Minus 3, 4 and 5), to gain access and manipulate your inherent good nature. Before long you will find yourself in the same negative states as them.

One of the biggest mistakes you can make is to believe, uncritically, that others are kind, reaffirming and rational. That path will lead you to fritter away many years of your life in the company of, and under the influence of, intensely negative people.

The Answer

First know this Scale Of Emotional and Social Health. Then choose your friends carefully, according to their real position on it. Those who sit below Plus 3 should be dumped unceremoniously. If you can't do so, because it's family or work colleagues, strictly minimize your contact and do not socialize with the lower types.

Secondly, get yourself fixed up with Punk Psychology®. You'll never be the same again. It's the only really profound way to release emotional charges from the past and find your freedom in the present, shedding old and destructive patterns, beliefs and feelings.

It's the best way by far to raise "Real IQ"! We use it to unlock the genius within.

Moreover, you can easily learn to do it for others and, for many, this has become a deeply fulfilling career or second career. It can be quite lucrative.

OK, let's move on now, maybe with a bit of history, to give some background to the new skills you'll be learning! Just don't let Freud and that crowd scare you. It's much simpler than they ever thought. And this is 21st century science, not medieval, Victorian and Aquarian New Age, all of which are now rendered obsolete!

CHAPTER 4

A BRIEF HISTORY OF MIND EXPLORATION

I believe all mind workers will be enriched in their knowledge and endeavors, if they take the trouble to acquire a little history! To that end, I here introduce a short section outlining the key historic advances, in the hope it will enrich, entertain and, above all, enlighten every such worker.

Nobel Laureate for Physics, Richard Feynman, near the start of his famous Feynman Lectures on Physics, posed an awesome question: What if, in some great cataclysm, all scientific knowledge were to be destroyed and only one sentence was to be passed on to future generations to help them? What statement would contain the most valuable information, in the fewest words (to allow them to re-discover everything pretty quickly for themselves, of course)?

Feynman answered his own question: *all things are made of atoms* (italics in the original). We know it's not that simple but it would give them a great start and save over two thousands years of enquiry!

What about a one-sentence psychology? What one, complete, sentence, would sum up the core of what we know about the mind and human behavior?

I'm going to choose this and then justify myself in due course: *Hidden memory has destructive effects while it remains hidden and is not self-correcting; conscious memory can be altered freely and is therefore not destructive, given that it is relevant.*

Of course the sciences of the mind are not nearly as crisp as physics, chemistry and medicine. So we can't expect something quite as clean and neat as Feyman's answer.

But I think the words emphasized are just about the number one fundamental of what has been learned so far about why people think, feel and behave as they do. Buried, or what we today call subconscious, memory is the origin of all our woes.

Let's go to some history and work back around to the real point of this tract and then I'll justify my chosen "heritage statement"!

The Growth Of Psychology and Psychiatry ················

If the physical treatment of disease was, since early times, pretty barbarous, then the treatment of mental illness has been even worse. So cruel, ignorant and without rationality was this branch of the medical arts that even by the nineteenth century it had advanced no further than bondage, gagging and whipping.

Inmates of mental institutions were often treated more savagely than interned criminals. I make the point that, just as Nazism has far from vanished today, this depraved and backward attitude in the healing profession has not suddenly gone away. It surfaces now in the desire to administer electric shocks to those in mental pain, or even to slash away part of their brains, in the crude and irreversible operation of lobotomy.

Do not think that just because the majority of members of the profession abhor the latter "treatment" that there is not a substantial lobby of those who want to see it re-instated. I view this as no different from the perversion of wanting to hurt and torment those who cannot defend themselves.

Is not the history of witch-hunting, burnings and torture a kind of demonic version of supposed healing of ills and the ridding of communal guilt and dis-ease by pain and brutality? I think it may be so.

Of course there has always been the enlightened element. Sadly, their voice was not strong. An early champion of reason was Juan Luis Vives, born in Valencia in 1492, the year Columbus made his landfall in America. Vives was later a friend of Desiderius Erasmus and Sir Thomas More and became professor of humanities at the Flemish university of Louvain.

Vives wrote profoundly and compassionately of what everyone else feared unto hysteric proportions and explained "demonic possession", as nothing more than a malady of the psyche. Vives' most important work *De Anima* (of the soul, which happens also to be the title of a tract by Aristotle) was probably the first study of major emotions and could be said to be the start of what we now call psychiatry (literally, medicine of the soul).

Johann Weyer (or Wier), a doctor born 1515 in North Brabant (now Netherlands), published a book in 1563 titled *De Praestigius Daemonum* and was an equally enlightened writer. He argued in a strikingly modern manner that most so-called witches were mentally disturbed, many of them due to mistreatment and abuse by their captors, rather than being inherently deranged or vicious. In his view it was the persecuting clergy who should be punished and not the unfortunate women they targeted as responsible for the world's ills.

Naturally, Weyer's book was denounced and placed on the infamous "Index" of books forbidden by the Catholic Church (and moreover it remained so until the beginning of the twentieth century).

In the same vein, I cannot resist mentioning my partial namesake, Reginald Scott, whose *Discoveries Of Witchcraft* also attempted to expose witch hunting as a fraud and cited actual examples of tricks and sleight of hand used to incriminate innocents. At a stroke he joined the founders of modern psychology but also made his mark as author of what the Magic Circle describes as virtually the first book to treat of conjuring, as we know it today.

[this whole section best referenced through E W F Tomlin, *Psyche, Culture And The New Science*, Routledge and Kegan Paul, London 1985, pps. 8- 9]

Mind As Therapy

It isn't possible to say how far back the idea of mental healing goes. Dream therapies in Ancient Rome and many similar primitive, semi-mystical approaches, some of which survive in aboriginal societies even today, could be considered to be of this type. Shamanism too, has overtones of this type of mind healing.

In modern times (in other words post-Newton), Anton Mesmer (1734—1815) could be considered the first person to approach healing via the mind. His theories were based on the notion of animal magnetism. By potentiating this mysterious quality he was able to induce trance-like states, which made the subjects very suggestible to cures.

It all sounded very dubious to his contemporaries but there is little doubt that he enjoyed enormous repute based on the fact that he achieved considerable success. People were willing to undertake long journeys and pay substantial fees to obtain his treatment.

Naturally, he was denounced by the medical profession of the day who then, as now, seemed more interested in protecting the status quo than furthering the pursuit of healing knowledge. Instead of learning from Mesmer, they put a stop to him. His star fell.

This remarkable figure lives on now chiefly in the word mesmerize, which is often used pejoratively for the act of deliberately bamboozling someone with mind tricks. Mesmerism is also often used interchangeably, though not strictly correctly, with hypnotism, a word coined by a British physician James Braid (1795—1860).

Medical Hypnotism

The first serious scientific attempt to investigate the mind and mentally caused (psychosomatic) ills came from that great and compassionate French physician and scientist Jean-Martin Charcot (1825—1893). He came to it almost by accident when, for a prank, two of his students hypnotized a woman and implanted in her the characteristics of an organic illness. When Charcot discovered the truth, though chagrined, he nevertheless realized the enormous significance of what he had witnessed.

The mind was capable of creating all the signs and symptoms of a full, somatic disease, without any real disease present.

Instead of dismissing the matter with a show of authoritarian pomposity, Charcot devoted most of his remaining years to using hypnotism to study what we now call psychosomatic illness. At that time the fashionable term was hysteria, though it had a rather different usage to that which we give it now. Even so, the sneering implications were there.

Etymologically, the word hysteria comes from the Greek for womb or uterus

(*hysteros*) and this reflects the belief of former times that a floating womb was the origin of this complaint. Charcot came under particular attack for daring to suggest that men might suffer from hysteria too; experts of the day not only considered this a ridiculous suggestion but a thoroughly obnoxious one.

I have often wondered who those two students were and whether they were aware that their practical joke made an enormous stride towards the breakdown of one of medicine's last great frontiers: understanding the mind in health and disease. After all, it was their playful idea!

It is hard for us in these more educated times to understand just how much in contempt psychosomatic illness was held by the medical profession until the mid-twentieth century. Even to study it was felt not quite proper and Charcot had to endure much scorn and abuse for daring to do so.

But all that was to change and largely due to the work of one man, who was himself a pupil of Charcot and learned the mysterious power of hypnotism from him: Sigmund Freud. Pierre Janet was a pupil of Charcot's too and I have already hinted that Freud liberally plagiarized Janet's work in what was to follow...

The Talking Cure

Freud's story has been told and re-told many times and need not delay us long.

The milestone book he published with his colleague Josef Breuer called *Studies in Hysteria* (Vienna 1893- 95) is arguably one of the greatest medical texts of all time (and one of the least read). With it, what may be called modern psychiatry really had its origins. A collection of startling case histories, it was in every sense a definitive book, a paradigm shift of the type Thomas Kuhn has described in *The Structure of Scientific Revolutions*. (T. S. Kuhn *The Structure of Scientific Revolutions*, University of Chicago Press, Chicago, 1970).

The two collaborators used hypnotism to penetrate deeply into the psyche of the individuals they studied and treated. For the first time, they were able to show that many strange outer manifestations of disease were nothing more than re-enactments, on the physical level, of traumatic memory, which had lain too deep to recall. We have grown so accustomed to this idea that it is difficult to grasp just what a breakthrough this meant at the time.

Perhaps the only thing which serves to remind us today, is reading about the tremendous furore its publication caused. Leading experts of the day were scandalized, appalled, shocked and, above all, incredulous and wasted no time in damning Freud and his theories, largely on a very bitter personal note.

To some extent he never lived down the acrimony and vituperation, though his notoriety lives on while most of his petty-minded critics are long forgotten.

One of the cases from the book, Anna 0. (a pseudonym), later became something of a celebrity in her own right.

It was she who described the treatment she had been having as "The Talking Cure" and the name simply stuck.

Dissipating The Memory

The essence of the treatment was called "abreaction" or catharsis, the dissipation or taking the sting out of traumatic memories by reliving them.

It is vital for success that the original feelings are contacted and re-experienced.

The patient would naturally talk it through as a narrative and it would indeed seem to a layperson as if chronic afflictions were being lifted simply by talking about them. Hypnotism facilitated the process, by parting the curtain, to reveal otherwise deeply buried and unavailable memories.

Eventually Freud and Breuer quarreled and fell apart, at least in part due to Freud's developing obsession with sexuality as the core of all motivation. Breuer was more cautious.

Note the similarities between "The Talking Cure" and religious confessional. It would be naïve to deny it.

Yet, all the major Western religious traditions—mainline Protestantism, Judaism, and the Catholic church—fought Freud's methods vehemently, steadfastly maintaining that only their rules had any merit, not the individual judgments informed by a conscience. Indeed, the 1832 decree of Pope Gregory XVI, had pronounced it "false and absurd, or rather mad, that we must secure and guarantee to each one liberty of conscience".

In this instance it was surely the crazy Pope talking heretical (and hysterical) nonsense. No-one today would support the old fool's notion that Mankind should be denied their freedom of individual conscience.

Psychoanalysis

Freud continued his researches alone and developed his revolutionary therapeutic approach, which he called psychoanalysis. Briefly, it is a piecemeal abreaction of hidden traumas. The patient talks freely about his or her life, especially the formative years of childhood. The therapist (analyst) notes what is being said, looking for clues to deeper material. In the meantime, little by little, pain is supposedly chipped away from these forgotten events, even though they may not be directly remembered.

It is a central hypothesis to psychoanalysis, that apparently "free" talk is in fact considerably guided by hidden areas of the mind (the subconscious). Thus, if the patient says enough over a sufficient period of time, he or she will eventually reveal their inner secrets and burdens (hidden, that is, even from themselves).

When the psychoanalyst has heard enough, he attempts a summary, pinpointing the source of the trouble and explaining it in a way which clothes it with rationality. This is called the synthesis. The great weakness of this method is that if the synthesis is wrong, the results are compromised at best—and could be disastrous.

Freud went on to elaborate many interesting theories about the mind and behavior, such as the Oedipus complex (boy's jealous hatred of his father as a rival for mother's love). The theories he expounded became ever more complicated, bizarre and sexual in nature.

In the liberalizing environment of the Twentieth Century this suited many but, eventually, his name has fallen into disrepute and he is now viewed somewhat derisorily as a peddler of smutty science and scatology.

Very little of Freud's writings finds favor today, except for their considerable historic interest.

However many of the words he coined, such as the ego and libido, have become part of our very language, though they are usually used without much understanding of the meaning he gave them.

Post-Freud

Since Freud's time many theories on the mind and behavior have been put forward.

He may have been mistaken in many of his notions but he unquestionably acted as a catalyst. Eventually, even those most moved and influenced by his ideas, Jung, Adler and others, found the dogmas too restricting and went their own separate ways, evolving new concepts and pursuing their own search for better therapies.

Yet even in contradiction, Freud's ideas exerted a powerful sway over others who followed and his patriarchy casts a long shadow that is still with us. Not that this is in any way meant to diminish the powerful writings of the Post-Freudians, as they are called, merely to say that without Freud there would have been no Jung, even though it is the latter who today enjoys the most popularity and esteem.

Sometimes the pendulum has swung too far. Men like Fritz Perls, famous in Gestalt circles, claimed to have "debunked" all of Freud, though probably gripped by more than a little ego-mania, to use an unkind Freudian expression! (Perls S F, *Gestalt Therapy Verbatim*, Real People Press, Lafayette (CA), 1969, p.1).

And Perls' words ring with increasing hollowness, as the decades pass. You may be able to get a balloon filled with hot air to rise but that doesn't mean you have debunked the law of gravity.

The fact is that, although Freud elaborated many concepts which were highly personalized and seem to us today to be unacceptable, even far-fetched, he passed on certain fundamental discoveries from Pierre Janet that were based on direct first-hand experience and there is no finer tool in the pursuit of scientific knowledge than personal insight.

These formative precepts are really found to be unassailable by anyone who takes the trouble to test them out properly. Without taking on board the complicated models, such as the id and alter-ego, I believe these core observations concerning the mind are as meaningful and inescapable as the germ-theory of disease or the laws of molecular biology.

I have taken the trouble to identify and list what I consider to be Freudian axioms, though Freud never described these as such and you won't find them referred to anywhere else. They are axioms in the sense they are self-evident truths, when viewed along the lines both Janet and Freud pursued in their research. You need to grasp them fully to become a competent practitioner of Punk Psychology®!

You need to grasp them fully to become a competent practitioner of Hypnoetics™!

Freudian Axioms

1. Memory is the mind's recording of past events, which happened to an individual, from the first moment of consciousness to the present (NOW).

2. Much of memory is hidden. The fact that it is hidden does not mean that it does not exist. Janet called this buried material subconscious memory and Freud adopted the term.

3. Subconscious memory is powerful. It retains the violence and force of original painful and counter-survival experiences. Time does not diminish this latent force, merely obscures it.

4. Hidden memory is the most destructive because it cannot be interpreted by reason. Subconscious memories can take control of conscious personality and force its imprint on thoughts, actions, dreams, phrases and other mental processes. In doing so, the subconscious mind does not reveal itself except by inference.

5. The conscious analytical personality will rationalize these unwanted actions, thoughts, emotions, dreams, phrases and other mental processes, without recognizing the true origin of them. It tries to "make sense" of what is happening.

6. Hidden memory can also evoke physical symptoms, such as pains, malfunctioning organs, and other signs of organic disease (psychosomatic illness).

7. If the buried memories can be contacted and experienced in a conscious, knowing way, their force diminishes and their hold over conscious processes is relieved.

8. One way to access such hidden memory is to re-experience it, as if it were NOW, undergoing feelings, thoughts and sensation within the original time reference. This is called abreaction or revivification.

9. Once contacted and re-experienced, these hidden memories return to normal conscious memory and are made available for rational thought processes.

10. The individual experiences a resurgence of self-determinism and freedom, in proportion to the quantitative release of hidden distressing memories.

11. Memory experiences tend to be associated in linear sequences, or "threads" or ropes; latest back to earliest. The first time it happened, or "root", is key to releasing negative effects.

12. The earliest time on a thread may not be available easily but will emerge as later events are abreacted, bringing the earliest or "root" into view. We call this unburdening.

All this is core to what we do in Punk Psychology™ and Hypnoetics™. If these twelve precepts don't seem obvious to you, then let me state that when you work with the mind and memory, seeking to release thoughts, feelings and behaviors from control by past events and decisions, you will see them at work 100% consistently.

Problems With The Psychoanalytical Model

Despite the core nature of these axioms, there is no escaping the fact that psychoanalysis has major limitations as a therapy. This indeed is the prime reason the movement splintered and has more or less foundered.

According to *Time* magazine (23rd Nov 1993), "Freud's reputation today has probably never been lower."

First attempts in any field can be stellar in magnitude, yet with the passage of time seem primitive. The first motor cars were pretty remarkable in their day but by present standards, their performance would be considered poor, even laughable. If no-one had questioned the weaknesses in design there would have been no advances.

However, there can also be too much "development" and then the fundamentals are in danger of being lost. It can be very difficult to strike a balance between unquestioning acceptance of old dogmas and radicalism to the point of failing to profit from hard-won experience—or even losing sight of it.

The problem with Freud's psychoanalysis is four-fold:

1. Firstly, it takes an inordinate length of time (perhaps years).

2. This means ultimately it is expensive, which is good for the analyst but not for the patient.

3.

4. Secondly, it is essentially unguided and the difficulty with problems in the mind is that we tend to shy from, and have trouble confronting, that which is most destructive and hurtful to us. In other words, that which would do us the most good is the least comfortable and, left to our own devices, we would tend to avoid it altogether.

5. Thirdly, synthesis is dangerous.

6. If the analyst gets it wrong (which is certainly often, since one cannot ever be sure what another person is thinking), the incorrect "explanation" of the person's troubles only adds to the problem by becoming a further confusion, which is then also part of the problem.

7. Finally, the interpretation becomes the excuse, not a real solution. Instead of being fully integrated, the patient sails through life with a reason to flaunt, which "explains" why they are not fully integrated.

What was needed was a workable approach to locating key memories and abreacting them properly, one for one, not disregarding memory as the major source of aberration and ills.

Obviously, progress would depend on a greater understanding of what was going on in the mind, how it was structured and how it functioned.

In the absence of that data, the subject languished somewhat.

New theories sprang up, which sought to evade the issue of subconscious memory and its effects, or at least to cope without any successful way of dealing with it.

So today we hear deprecation of what are loosely termed regression therapies (or sometimes called "historic work"). The reason that so-called regression therapy often appears ineffective is more a question of poor therapeutic technique than any weakness in the basic precepts. Practitioners cannot seem to keep their own case out of the way and insist on interrupting, explaining, correcting, interpreting and otherwise adding to the client's story, all of which is counter-productive.

Moreover, when figures like Wagner Bridger, erstwhile president of the Society for Biological Psychiatry, in a report in the July 1969 *Clinical Psychiatry News* declared that personality is in no way affected by childhood and there is no relationship between early experience and adult outcome, we realize that science, or the fashion that dominates science of the day, can at times be very, very silly.

If true, this proposition effectively severs an individual from his or her own history.

Clearly to doctors who share this view there is no such thing as the past; we do not grow up a composite of our experiences. Someone raised in the South who hates blacks presumably has a bad gene and did not acquire this antisocial attitude from listening to parents, peers and other adults around him in his childhood.

A serial killer must have been potentially dangerous, even as a child, since he was born that way and not warped by some tormenting occurrence in his formative years. Indeed, according to Bridger and his like, there are no formative years!

What The Punk Psychology® Practitioner Knows ·······

Anyone conversant with Punk Psychology® is fully capable of techniques to bring about release from past psychic traumas, using a modern "plastic memory" approach that is far more effective than a mere abreaction-style approach. He or she knows it is unkind to leave someone stuck in a past event.

Individuals can become so mired into the impact of an event that he or she cannot move forward in time. They remain "stuck" to the past. In a sense they are so tuned to the past and unavailable for the present that their state is somewhat zombie-like, or somnambulistic to use Janet's term, which is to say: having little consciousness present in the here and now. He or she is in a trance or dream state but will react, eat, sleep, even talk, as a travesty of normalcy.

Compassion requires that we release them wherever possible and it is rather easy to do. The Punk Psychology® practitioner has no problem with this. Hopefully, you will now see why my one-sentence synopsis of human emotions and behavior will save centuries of re-investigation, in the event that all our current knowledge is lost!

Let's leave our history and move on to theory and practice.

Punk Points

- Memory is powerful. It can create strange emotions, behaviors, patterns and thoughts.

- Memory can even provoke real organic disease and sometimes imitations of it (psychosomatic symptoms).

- It causes the most trouble when it is hidden (so-called subconscious memory). The person concerned does not know the origin of their strange emotions, behaviors, patterns and thoughts.

- If the buried memories can be contacted and experienced in a conscious, knowing way, their force diminishes and their hold over conscious processes is relieved.

- The individual feels better and better, with a quantitative resurgence of self-determinism and freedom, in proportion to the release of hidden distressing memories.

CHAPTER 5
WHAT IS A MIND?

We might start with asking a very punky question: *what is a mind?* I doubt that any psychiatrist or psychologist could give a definition that has much meaning or practical value. The mind tends to be something of a mystery.

We all have a mind (well, except politicians). So you would think there is a common understanding of what a mind is and what it's supposed to do. This knowledge I find singularly lacking.

In fact we should maybe ask a more basic question first: *is there such a thing as a mind?* Or is it what B F Skinner, the great American behavioral psychologist, described as an "explanatory fiction"?

He said we're all robots, which just throw out behaviors, only behaviors, and that thoughts, feelings, intentions, dreams and motivations are all illusions. We only think we have intentionality. That really we are no more "there" and in control of our lives than a robot programmed to respond unthinkingly to stimuli input.

This is called behaviorism. Because all you can see is the behavior, therefore that's all there is! I doubt Skinner thought this of himself, when he was sitting down to dinner with a family. But who knows?

Things have progressed little today. We have a science that thinks everything is brain; that actions are predetermined and that thoughts follow actions, or follow light up signals in the brain. It can't be the other way round, they say, since we can see the electrical signals light up a split second before the person even has the thought.

But that's silly. There is preparatory thought, before that which is consciously grasped and verbalized. We see that all the time using our eMind Sensor™ (GSR meter). End of problem.

See, Skinner was talking about people—masses—populations. He wasn't looking inwardly; he was *observing other people,* outwardly. We as individuals know that we have a mind and we have thoughts, feelings, intentions and so forth. We choose what we know and what we do. That's not to say we are not influenced by hidden factors within, but we still have choices, awareness and what they call "agency", meaning we do it for ourselves; we are not pre-programmed automatons (even though at times we look as if we are).

So let's start from there.

Even with this supposition, we have some big questions. I have already disposed of the argument that the mind *must be* located in the brain. But we can see that *part of* mental functioning is controlled by brain activity.

The brain is our powerful "bio-computer", if you like. But like all computers, it needs an operator at the interface, to work the controls. These days I have even started to add the rhetorical question: is a smart phone a part of our mind? It has memory and output. That's isn't so different from some of our mental computations, like remembering stuff and having the power to know where we are (as with the phone's GPS functions).

Computers and The Mind

Perhaps we can widen the consideration to the possibility that all computer storage, computation and retrieval devices are part of our "extended mind". We dip in and out of the data banks, to recover information, much as we do when we are trying to mentally recall something we learned.

Some people, as you know, are even predicting that computers will eventually rival the human mind. These are the so-called "strong" artificial intelligence (AI) proponents.

But this runs out of steam very quickly. Computers, at this time, are pretty simple, even if vast in scale: if A and B, then C type calculations; or if A and NOT B, then D, type logic. The human mind is far more complex than this.

It's true, computers have moved on to fuzzy logic and "soft" computing, which more closely matches the workings of the mind, abandoning the yes-no logic in favor of something greyer and more reasonable.

But no computer to date has come even close to the capabilities of the human mind. Consider:

We have almost infinite capacity to remember. We don't use it all in everyday thinking but research makes it very clear that everything we experience is recorded at some level or other, even if we selectively choose to not remember it all, or at least we select not to be consciously aware of, most of it.

I couldn't give any accurate figures but the amount of data storage we would use up before we even became adults would probably be in the region of squillions of gigabytes of data. No machine can do that, though I accept they can get better and better at storage.

Computers are, of course, famous for accuracy and speed. But the human mind, I believe (with reason), also makes 100% accurate calculations *based on the data it is fed*. When we behave badly, do stupid things or get inappropriate emotions, that's just because the mind is working on faulty input.

In other words, given what the calculation is based on, the mind is accurate to perfection. To get better outcomes from your thoughts and behavior, all you have to do is tune up the data and work only with good data. I'll be talking more about that later. But let me just say that that's what Hypnoetics™ is all about.

The human mind is self-correcting. It's true; computers are learning these skills to a degree. But a computer cannot go through its past history and re-write everything in the light of new experiences or new evaluations. The human mind does this all the time.

Indeed, we would not be human if it didn't. We can investigate past experience, decide we were wrong and rewrite our entire data banks in the light of the new perspective. That's what we do, routinely, with Hypnoetics™ mastery.

The big difference between a computer and the mind is that the mind needs no external programmer; computers have not reached that stage. Computers which program themselves have been programmed to program themselves! That's nowhere near comparable in magnitude to what the mind does.

The mind can not only program itself but it can take its programming intention from the circumstances it finds itself in. Further, the mind can determine what determinants to judge by (values) and so choose what would be the most optimum outcomes in a given situation and so organize action towards that chosen end.

But then it could decide against that same chosen end, pick another one, and then re-program the entire mind to proceed in the new direction. And it can do this, make everything change, in less than a second.

There's another big difference between us and current computers: a busted computer needs a human to fix it. Don't tell me the latest and greatest will be able to do that for itself. Where is it going to buy (yes, buy) the cables and chips it needs to effect a repair?

The human mind has the capacity to take in remote information and evaluate its worth. It can accept input as visual (photo, video), audio (sound recordings) and text analysis (reading). Computers can accept this kind of input, of course. But they cannot yet evaluate such input. A computer is not aware of what it receives as video, for example, even though a computer can be programmed to at least partially understand and respond to visual (cameras).

So a computer could replicate a picture of a naked woman, say. But it cannot think "dirty whore", or "She's beautiful, I think I'm in love!" In the same way, a computer does not have the consciousness to think, "I'm lonely, I wish there were another computer around here I could link up with."

Now strong-AI supporters think it is only a matter of time before this happens. Strong-AI thinks that everything in the human mind is just algorithms. That's a fancy word meaning a series of steps, with several stages of input; a manipulation which transforms those things; and comes out with a relevant output (input, step 1, step 2, step 3, output), kind of progression.

The Turing Test

The question is: can computers ever simulate human thought processes. What do you think?

Men have been trying to design a computer smart enough to mimic human thought for over half a century. It's called the Turing test, after British mathematician Alan Turing (made famous in the code breaker movie *The Imitation Game*, starring Benedict Cumberbatch). There's a prize for the first person to come up with a computer that can simulate being human. As of the time of writing this, nobody has succeeded, though there are claims from time to time (the 2014 claim for a program called Eugene Goostman is widely considered not credible).

The rules are pretty tough: a computer is set up in competition with a human being; each gives its replies in an identical format (usually digital type on the screen); an investigator asks questions and has to guess from the replies whether he or she is dealing with a machine or a real live human [Turing, A.M. (1950). Computing machinery and intelligence. *Mind*, 59, 433-460].

It's conceivable that some day a machine will pass this test. You could put it in terms that a computer can "think". It still doesn't mean that a computer is conscious. A sufficiently complex computer, with algorithms and complex movements, could even be designed one day, to behave like a human being.

That still doesn't mean the computer is conscious.

But here's the killer:

To be able to compete with a human mind, a computer is also going to have to have imagination. This faculty does not just mean the ability to create visionary futures. Even the crudest computers can do that. What is really meant by imagination is the ability to create something out of nothing, meaning; *totally unrelated to anything which has ever existed before.*

No Newtonian computer is going to come up with the Theory of Relativity, because the leap into a completely new reality is beyond a machine, which only knows one existing reality. Imagination is the main point at which computers fall down.

Throw in things like out-of-body experiences and previous incarnations and the notion of conscious, self-aware computers becomes just a dud concept. These phenomena, unfortunately for the AI enthusiasts (and psychologists), seem to be real. At least they occur over and over to normal, intelligent, rationally functioning human beings. Not everyone who experiences this degree of self-awareness is deluded, believe me.

Awareness of Being Aware ·····································

There is a famous problem in philosophy and consciousness studies; it's called "The Zombie Problem". The discussion is about theoretical zombies, so don't worry: you won't have to go digging up corpses and reviving them to learn about this aspect of theory!

But a zombie, for this discussion, is somebody walking around, talking and eating, like you and me, but isn't conscious. Or at least, is not self-aware.

This is not a crazy idea; a robotic kind of flesh zombie would know to eat, not to get wet when it rained, would like one food more than another and (probably) would try sex, although it might be a bit rough on the partner!

The zombie would *seem* to be behaving like you and me; but is walking around in an unknowing dream. A somnambulist trance, in other words. How could you tell it was conscious or not? Kick it and it screams is not enough: any animal, and maybe even plants, react negatively to pain stimuli.

Talk to it and get the right answer doesn't prove anything either.

The amusing point is, a lot of people are going around as if they are zombies. At least they make few or no self-aware comments, like "I think I am..." or "I see myself doing..."

Most people don't get above "I love burgers..." or "I *hate* Paris Hilton..." or "My feet ache..."

Some of you might at least suspect, humans seem to be having a psychical relationship with their electronic toys, such as the way people interact with their iPhone etc. It's like nobody is home. You see people with their phone clamped to their ear (often while driving), as if they don't even see themselves existing, unless somebody wants to talk to them. They seem to need the comfort of something going in their ears, to reassure themselves they are alive in some way! It's all rather weird.

Anyway, the point about the zombie problem is that there really is no easy way to tell if a person is conscious or not. Ask one if it likes pop music, the taste of hot dogs...

You'll get yes and no responses, the same as you would with an aware, self-aware human being. There is nothing in most human interactions that would tell you that a zombie understands why they like some thing or not others, or where their opinions come from.

A computer could pass the Turing Test and yet still remain nothing more than an electronic zombie.

Conscious vs. Unconscious Processing

Having said all that, let me say this: part of our thought processes clearly go on at an algorithmic level. I think it's fair to say that the unconscious mind works algorithmically. I agree with Roger Penrose, who says that it may go on at a complicated high level, which is monstrously difficult to disentangle in detail. But it does seem a computer-like automaticity. The unconscious mind, or subconscious, is an automaton.

But again, he says that conscious thought can also be algorithmic, but at a very different level of organization. He doesn't say so but isn't that what we mean by "logic": accurate algorithmic processing but in the full light of consciousness?

It's good because logic is one of our very powerful faculties. Intuition and magic are fine, in their way. But it's logical thought that got us down from the trees, building cars, computers and space rockets!

And this still leaves a large part of consciousness capacity that isn't explained. The riddle comes from the fact that *thinking is not the same consciousness.* They co-exist but are not to be confused.

The Real You

Now, let's roll on towards a working definition of the mind, which is the real purpose of this chapter. This is what I used to teach; it's still true—but it's not true enough, as we shall see!

The important thing about observing yourself is that the observer is the real you. What you are observing is not you. You are the watcher, the observer, the entity in the driving seat.

We call that entity our consciousness or self. It's the faculty of being aware and being aware of being aware. Beyond that, nobody has a clue what consciousness actually is or how it arises in the first place.

I use the metaphor of *the knife which cannot cut itself:* consciousness cannot examine itself. It just is!

Now there is a slight complication here, which is that there are really multiple "selves". The idea of a single conscious unity or just a single "You" is untenable today. It's pretty obvious that we have parts. I could go on to mention psychic "entities" out there but let's keep this simple for now.

So, how am I going to sum up what a mind is? That was my promise from the title, after all.

The mind is a functional interface between consciousness and exterior reality. Now I say "exterior reality" not meaning that to be confined only to the physical universe. There are other possible universes; lots of them. Or I should say other realities, because the word "universe" means "everything that is", so by definition there cannot be more than one universe; only variations in reality and appearance.

Even fuddy-duddy science today is taking about multiple universes, so there is nothing new or spooky about that.

There is still mystery in this, like how perceptions from physical organs, such as eyes and ears, reach consciousness. And also how something immaterial like consciousness can affect material things, like brain cells and neural pathways, to make them perform as they do.

There is this very important question of perception. Nothing is more disappointing than the way modern scientists, like Daniel Dennett, equate consciousness with perception. It's nuts! The zombie perceives but, as we have already seen, doesn't necessarily know it perceives, or what the perceptions really mean.

Studying how perceptions take place completely side-steps the big question raised by Bishop George Berkeley in the 18th century: *how can we be sure there is any universe out there at all?* Surely, all we know about is what our senses describe to us? We are jumping to unjustified conclusions to suppose that our senses are based on something that's out there. Maybe there is nothing; just senses and perceptions; or just ideas about something out there?

This position was shared by John Hulme and a fellow doctor called John Locke. He was among philosophers called the "British Empiricists" because they all came to the same conclusion: we can't know much about the world "out there" (if there is one) because the only way we can access it is via sensory perceptions, which are a function of the brain, not a function of what's "out there".

So our "world" is not a world but composite perceptions of a world! That's what they were saying. And, you know what? In two centuries, this has never been refuted; just argued about.

I don't want to bog down in this side-road of philosophy but the confusion between issues of perception and matters of true consciousness remains the biggest roadblock in the modern study of real consciousness.

The Mind's Number One Algorithm

So, if the mind is our interface, between us and reality, what does it DO exactly?

Actually, I think I can sum up the primary algorithm of the mind in one full sentence. The mind works with perceptions to scan the present time environment, to assess what is happening, which is then compared to past learning and experience, and from that future estimations are made, decisions formed, and appropriate action taken to proceed towards an optimum re-positioning, or what we would term an outcome.

You will see this is not the *reactive* mind of the physiologist or psychologist. This is the *proactive* mind at work. There is something beyond the mere stimulus-response level; a creativity, design and intention that takes us out of the merely animal and protoplasm level.

In our conscious life, we don't just react to things; we have our own little activities, games, plans and purposes. We don't just want to "survive" or stick around. We want better. The highest purpose in the universe, in my opinion, is benign self-fulfillment (benign, of course, because we don't want to harm others).

Now that is far from selfish gains for self. Writing elsewhere I have described our 12 Channels Of Being. That thought structure says that you cannot enhance one Channel at the expense of all others and expect a good result. It says that what is good for you is good for everyone and everything. The best you, is the best that this present reality could have.

Enlightened self-interest

The fullest concept of self-enhancement includes comprehensive positive activity and gratification in all 12 Channels Of Being. That's a very big concept and would fit only a super hero or living fireball, one who was capable of immense influence and activity. I'm talking about taking responsibility for all of creation and one's personal engagement with the totality of What-IS!

I'm talking about using your mind as a powerhouse to get not just anything you want but everything you can imagine. The power of the human mind has barely been explored. There are tantalizing clues as what the possibilities are; but it's obvious that most of us are living way below our full potential.

That's where Hypnoetics™ comes in: it's a path to formidable mental expansion. It is already pushing back the boundaries of thought, knowledge and successful behaviors.

It's what the world needs today... it's what we all need, desperately.

Punk Points: ··

- The mind is not a computer, though there are similarities, which make comparisons useful.

- Behaviorism is not enough. Behavior demands an explanation.

- The mind is continuously scanning the NOW, comparing it to learning and experience (memory), to predict what will happen next and so make favorable adaptations.

- Consciousness just IS. We can't really see it or inspect it.

CHAPTER 6

HOW DOES IT GO WRONG?

Let's go back to computers and a powerful property of computers, shared by the human mind, and which is critical: a computer doesn't make mistakes. If a computer gets it wrong, it's always because some kind of glitch crept in; in other words, there is a reason. If the data is correct and the algorithm is uninterrupted, then the answer which comes out is always correct, to as many decimal places as you programmed it.

So if this human mind is so great and perfect, compared to a computer, why does it keep screwing up? Ah, good question.

The answer, as I hinted, is that depends what the mind uses to compute with. If there is faulty input, there will be faulty output. If you are programmed with 2+2=7, you are never going to get any good answers to calculations, are you? If your mind programming told you that, "All blondes are gold diggers," you would start to act oddly, wouldn't you, especially around women?

Of course human reactions are not simple, as I have been explaining. But consider 2+2=7 as a metaphor for anything that goes wrong: "Problems with the opposite sex", "Hates authority", "Useless at communication", "Lousy self-image", "Resorts to unnecessary violence," "Insists on making a living by stealing from others," "suicide to further a twisted religious cause" or whatever happens to be the non-optimum situation.

In fact there are two main ways that the mind can get it wrong. Either bad data or a faulty process of reasoning—a corrupted algorithm. Let's start with bad data. It's back to the computer model of GI-GO (garbage in-garbage out); if you put in bad stuff, rubbish will come out the other end, no matter how brilliant the computer.

We collect tons of trashy learning in our lives. What follows here is a fast rundown how this gets into our thought processes. You will learn later in Supernoetics® how to manage data correctly, including what we call *information gating* (To gate: to put restrictions on what is allowed into your mind, by swinging the gate against what is undesirable or even harmful data, and opening it to let in what is of proven value).

How Data Impacts Thinking $\cdots\cdots\cdots\cdots\cdots\cdots\cdots\cdots\cdots\cdots\cdots\cdots\cdots$

We assume we think only clear, sensible, uncontaminated thoughts. At least everyone believes that of their own mind. But we do not. Scads of computational debris gets into our thinking processes, some of it is merely faulty information, which we absorbed innocently and unknowingly. Most of it is coming from deep within the subconscious mind.

Let's take the first. Being taught useless or false data is how kids and youngsters are mentally corrupted. The source of this mental garbage, typically, is adults! Children are filled with silly or destructive "facts" by the grown ups around them: parents, teachers, family and authority figures, notably religious leaders.

If you go through life believing something is true, because you were told it is, but it is NOT true, you are computing with bad data. Of course, all it takes to correct this is a revision of your information. Once you find out the true facts, then you can correct the erroneous data and start getting better outcomes.

The more destructive sort of bad data is that which resides in the unconscious mind. I'll come to that shortly.

Let's just neat away the conscious data stuff. There are a few ways that false data can creep into our thinking, without our realizing:
- Faulty perceptions
- Faulty education
- Unreliable sources
- Memes

Faulty Perceptions

This can be dismissed fairly quickly. But it seems obvious that if you *think* you saw wasn't so, then you will have poor outcomes using that data.

There can be a whole range of these confusions, like Schiaparelli believing he saw canals on Mars (but didn't), down to an infant believing they saw Momma "attacked" by Daddy (which they did see but the explanation was sex, not violence).

Even normal perceptions are notoriously unreliable. It's almost an axiom that if you have six witnesses to an accident, there will be six different versions of what actually happened.

The key point here is that the intention is for truth. The person honestly believes what they saw.

Faulty Learning

Since what we know (or think we know) is of such crucial importance, I have spent some time building up a classification of information. You'll meet these again in other Supernoetics® writings. I call these my Orders Of Knowledge (I also have the Orders Of Truth, which we'll meet later; these are very powerful). Let's take a look at these Orders Of Knowledge:

• Verified data (you've checked it and it's true)

• Unverified (not been checked and proven)

First comes verified data. Verified means checked as true (Latin: stem of *verax* = true). That means something you know and have learned or evaluated and decided is correct, *from personal experience*. This is the most valuable knowledge of all. It's pure gold. If you know it to be true and it works for you, it's proven. It doesn't matter whether it came from school or learned from life, if you tested it and it's correct, then it's valuable.

It remains your own truth, even if nobody else agrees. As Buddha said, "If it's true for you, then it's true."

Unverified

In contrast to that, we have unverified data. This means you haven't proven it for yourself. That's not to say a datum is wrong, only that it might be. So there is uncertainty about it. You can't trust the information. That makes it far less valuable as knowledge. Consider a car that might start sometimes, or it might not. You can imagine the frustrations. Well, that's about what you experience using unverified data!

You read something in a newspaper about the threat of war; it might be true, it might not be. What are you going to do? Draw out all your savings and flee to another territory? It would be unwise to act on data of this order.

Note that this has nothing to do with the opinions of others; so if you have been told orthodox medical treatment is the way to go, but you have had a bad experience and found alternative remedies better, then what you know to be true, for yourself, is what is true. It doesn't matter how many other people or government inspectorates say otherwise: alternative medicine works and orthodox medicine is a bad experience. That's what you have verified.

Unverified knowledge can come from a number of sources:
- School
- Authority
- Books
- Television
- Peers
- Internet
- Memes

School seems obvious. As a source of learning, it leaves a lot to be desired. In fact in places like the USA, it can be considered a failure, the outcomes are so bad.

Schools (and colleges) tend to rely in "authorities": people they consider important and beyond reproach. That's a very dangerous position to take.

If Professor Blodwlt of The Uckashuggum State University says hysteria is caused by a loose womb and therefore only affects women; that doesn't make it true! They said the Earth was flat; they said heavier-than-air machines would never fly; they said malaria was caused by "bad air"! They were wrong!

Big authorities are a bad way to get your data, actually.

This came home to me in my life and my medical skills. I discovered the power of food allergies. But professors and other "leading authorities" said there was no such thing. They even said I should not be allowed to talk about food allergies, it was so wickedly wrong to teach people that there was such a thing.

But I evaluated the data for myself, found it to be wonderfully true and workable. So I became one of the world's leading experts and among the top dozen doctors in the world, for that particular specialty. That's how powerful it can be, to do your own evaluation.

But books too can be wrong; television almost always is; and peers... well, forget it! Can you remember what your pals said about sex, before you found out for yourself?

Today the Internet stands for a monument of intellectual confusion and factual garbage. There are some reliable facts out there, but not many. You may perhaps have thought that Wikipedia is a good source. It's edited by the people, isn't it?

Not any more! People have had their editorship revoked for even writing about subjects that are considered erroneous by the "Thought Police". You couldn't now submit an article about the electric universe, for example. It conflicts with the Big Bang and is therefore wrong, say the authority sources. Homeopathy has been heavily attacked, despite centuries of workability and plenty of good scientific studies, which are being added to, even as I write. Now the homeopathy entry is locked to any revisions and it says, "Homeopathy is a pseudoscience – a belief that is incorrectly presented as scientific." They just ignore all the studies which show it works!

Call that knowledge?

Memes (Thought Viruses)

I have already referred to the seminal work of Richard Semon and his book *The Mneme* first published in 1904, though my George Allen & Unwin (London) edition is 1921).

The word mneme, from the Greek for memory, lives on. Today, we spell it differently (meme) and sometimes refer to it as a "thought virus", which is a good metaphor. It does rather seem like a thought or idea goes around, "infecting" one mind after another.

That's because memes are very often faulty. They are more examples of those, kind of, "everybody knows that..." thoughts, that are actually rarely valuable and often very destructive. "Destroy America" is a thought virus that's spreading in the world today.

Of course "Jesus is the son of God" is just a meme. It's a 2,000-year old thought virus that has spread successfully from person to person. I mean, true or not, it isn't written in the stars or carved immutable in the sides of the Himalayan mountains! It's just an idea passed from person to person, verbally and in writing. You can opt in to it, or not. Therefore it's a meme.

Parents might infect their children with an anti-semitic meme, or a poverty meme (all money is evil); or mother constantly screams "You filthy pervert'" at the father and the daughter grows up believing this for the rest of her life. Maybe father had only suggested sex in something other than the missionary position.

Hypnotism Provides Some Clues

Of far more consequence than addled learning and education is the way the algorithmic function of the mind gets scrambled. We now come to some of the punk, dark mechanisms of the mind that literally and totally screw us up! This is the 2+2=7 cookie.

To gain an understanding, consider this important working model:

A stage hypnotist asks for a volunteer; a young woman comes up willingly. The hypnotist uses his "fluence" on her and she is soon in a daze.

He implants into her the suggestion that every time he touches his tie, she will come to him and kiss him. He says, "You will not remember this. But when I click my fingers, you'll wake up and everything will be normal."

He then wakes her up. He touches his tie and she rushes over to kiss him. The audience roars with laughter; they know the secret. But the woman does not. She's puzzled about the laughter. "I couldn't help myself, you're such a good looking guy," she whispers to the hypnotist!

He thanks her for volunteering and then touches his tie again. She kisses him again. The crowd roars. Now, if she is lucky, the hypnotist will bring her out of this trance and send her home safely. However, many volunteers for this sort of mind circus are not so lucky. They spend months or years unable to sleep properly or settle down. They feel deeply disturbed but without knowing what it is that's troubling them.

In our example, the girl may keep wanting to kiss strange men. She's knows this is bad, maybe even dangerous, but can't help herself. She is totally unaware that it is a man touching his tie that triggers her weird desire.

This case is an example of what is called post-hypnotic suggestion. The person is rendered lightly unconscious or "suggestible" and an idea or command is dropped into the mind, which is then buried by a blanking buffer, such as, "When you wake up, you will not remember this."

The MILLION DOLLAR question is: *can life do this to you, as a natural course of events?* In other words, does life work the same mechanism as post-hypnotic suggestion, without a hypnotist involved?

The answer is a whole-hearted YES.

In fact we carry on board hundreds, if not thousands, of naturally installed suggestions and crazy ideas. Some have powerful command impact over us. They literally dictate behaviors that we would rather not engage in... but we can't stop ourselves from doing certain things.

It's like being permanently hypnotized and walking around in a trance. The trance is somnambulism, to use the 19th century term.

We scream at the wife, kick the cat, abuse the kids or neighbors, overeat to the point of obesity and sickness, suffer endless headaches, or drink and drive recklessly. You can compile your own list of crazy humanoid behaviors. They are all irrational and all have one key characteristic, which is that the person cannot help him or herself. They are driven by some unknown force.

The person doesn't know why they do what they do. The origins of the implanted thoughts, emotions or behaviors are buried from conscious view; some deeper than others, of course, but none are understood by the person concerned.

In fact later, you will learn a Hypnoetics™ rule: as soon as the moment of origination of a thought, emotion or behavior is brought up into the conscious light of day and is fully inspected, the problem vanishes completely. The person comes to an understanding of the moment they became "hypnotized". As a result, the muddled thoughts, with their accompanying emotions and behaviors, drop away miraculously, as with the example of the fear of cats already described.

This is quite remarkable.

Meet The Reptilian Brain

You might wonder how all the crazy thoughts and resulting problems are able to successfully take over and force us to experience and do things we would rather not, such as making the girl who had an uncontrollable desire to kiss a man who touched his tie.

Why can't we use common sense to override these buried implants in the mind?

There is no question, I believe, that it's a mechanism that was once extremely valuable to us in our evolution. We were protected by these overriding responses. Like a gazelle that smelled a whiff of lion, we would react instantly. Only those who did react unthinkingly remained alive to breed and evolve!

Scientists sometimes equate this un-thinking thinking, or reflex reactions, with the so-called reptilian brain. It's crude, beyond control and is very limited. There are NO choices.

Unfortunately, we are still stuck with this reflex or "reductionist" thinking.

I'm talking about a very low level of thought processes that Alfred Korzybski called "identification thinking", in which everything was run together in one thought blob: sort of X=Y=Z thinking, when clearly that is not true.

Korzybski had another term for this: UN-sanity. Not quite insanity. It reflects the fact that people are not generally insane. But each of us is, to some degree or other, insane about some small thing, whether that's claustrophobia, hatred of ethnic groups, viciously bad-tempered, inept as study and learning, sex crazy, wildly addicted or just plain stupid about certain matters.

Richard Semon, who I have already referred to, gives a great illustration of this natural insanity and how it is built up. His example is a dog, watching boys at play. One boy bends down and picks up a stone; he throws it at the dog and it hits home. Ouch! The dog is far from happy and runs for cover, where it sits licking its wound.

Weeks later that same animal sees a different boy bend down for some reason and runs off yelping in terror. It even feels the pain of the previous stone throwing injury.

But there is nothing to be afraid of. The second boy was simply bending down to tie his shoelaces. The dog went into the X=Y=Z computation mode and came up with the faulty idea that bending down, equals stone, equals pain, equals: *run while you can!*

An unpleasant event of the kind that Semon was describing we call a *memoneme*. More of that in the next chapter. Meanwhile, be sure to grasp that this is a mental override circuit, something where an instant protective reaction is called forth. No time to think. In the case of the dog, it didn't wait to see if this was going to be another stone throwing episode. It went into full overload, without time to reflect or reason sensibly.

We humans do this very often, as you will readily agree.

And like the dog, we have no obvious recall of the earlier memory. It happens anyway, without us being consciously aware of why we react as we do. Hence the term reductionist thinking (X=Y=Z).

You will see now that the core protocol of Hypnoetics™, which is to clear the timeline of buried memonemes, will have immeasurable benefit to the individual. Even without eradicating them all, we expect a tremendous resurgence on wellbeing, delight and mental clarity. The person will be more present (in the Now). We are working towards that spotless memory.

Trying to drag yourself into the Now, without a full understanding and cleansing of the mechanism by which you are trapped in the past (somnambulist), seems a difficult idea. Occasional success doesn't make it easy.

You will also perhaps appreciate why many populist psychologies, such as EFT and the Sedona Method (a version of Lester Levenson's "Releasing") are doomed to fail ultimately. Simply chanting "I feel fine," wherever you tap on your body, is no different to affirmations. It's not true; it's just something you wish was true.

Releasing or letting go of the idea, "I'm no good"—if you have a memoneme, with implanted commands, which conflicts with what you want to believe about yourself—well, guess which thought process will win?

You can't beat the lizard brain.

But you can flood it with knowing and understanding.

Punk Points:

- The mind works flawlessly, processing whatever data it is given in an accurate and useful manner.

- If the mind is fed faulty or conflicting data, it ceases to deliver worthwhile thoughts, emotions and behaviors, while nevertheless, doing the best it can with what it believes is right.

- Faulty or conflicting data can come from bad experiences (memonemes), which are subsequently buried from conscious view, or from numerous sources of faulty learning.

- Faulty learning comes from crazy education, parental nuttiness, popular memes (thought viruses), the Internet and social media, and arbitrary "authorities", such as educational leaders who are—quite frankly and literally—dangerous.

- Reductionist think (reptilian brain) is a very low level rightness, where many items that are dissimilar are not recognized as such, but instead identified with one another: X=Y=Z or UN-sanity, according to Alfred Korzybski.

CHAPTER 7

TERMINOLOGY AND STRUCTURES

OK, we are now working towards teaching you how to transform yourself, family and friends, using a simple introspection technique (*introspection:* looking inwards; the examination or observation of one's own mental and emotional processes).

First we need some terms and good definitions. Without adequate understanding of the elements involved, you are not likely to get satisfactory results. Punk doesn't mean notional or crazy; it just means challenging or counter to the general belief (notional: *existing only in theory or as a suggestion or idea*).

Piloting: the act of helping another by steering him or her in the direction of significant events in their personal history and taking steps to drain off the dark mental energy or "charge". This releases unpleasant emotions, negative beliefs, destructive decisions and unhelpful behaviors.

The Pilot: a person who has learned how to do this. You, the reader, if you follow guidance carefully.

Breakout: a specific time frame set aside for piloting, lasting an agreed length of time, free of all distractions. A breakout is entirely for the client's benefit and is *performed for no other reason*.

The Client: the person we are trying to help. He or she trusts the pilot and is willing to surrender control. However, at no time is the client unconscious or unaware. He or she is in a light introverted, relaxed state we call *alpha*. This is not a medical, psychiatric, therapeutic, or hypnotic state. It's something we all do, several times an hour! We also pass through alpha on the way to sleep and on the way back. It's nothing out of the ordinary.

Case: the sum total of the person's non-optimum thoughts, disagreeable emotions and self-limiting behaviors. Case is really the entirety of a person's character make-up. However, we mainly use it to denote the negative aspects of a person's psyche and behaviors.

Charge: Negative emotional energy embedded in past memories or future projections. We use the term charge, because life is basically an electrical state. We can detect charge on an electrical galvanic skin response meter (psycho-feedback meter). This is not to state that charge is an electrical phenomenon. Charge is actually a disturbance in consciousness and is best thought of as non-material mental energy or ruffled consciousness, that can be detected by changes in material measurements.

The Timeline: the sequential memory recordings of a person's experiences, from first awakening till now. Hermann Minkowski (1864-1909) coined the term "world path" as part of his mathematical model of the universe. A person's timeline is a more intimate and personal version of this world path.

Total Timeline (TT). The experiences a being has had in this and any other universe. It includes all past lives. We say a case has "gone TT" when he or she is able to travel freely beyond this lifetime.

Future Pacing. Taking the term "pacing" from NLP, future pacing means to investigate the future by laying it out as it might be, or the client would like it to be, and "experiencing" it as intended, to test its impact and significance.

MIMPs: this is short for mental imprints, or what we would ordinarily call a memory. M-ental im-age p-ictures for some individual—but remember not everyone sees memory in a visual way.

Usually we are aware of episodic memory, meaning recall of specific events, places and happenings that are linked together and not necessarily connected to other episodes or MIMPs. MIMPs seem extraordinarily accurate as to narrative, sights, audio (sounds and voices), emotion, physiology and a host of other factors that were part of the recorded episode. It seems likely that the timeline is made up of a continuous string of MIMPs.

[The other kind of memory is learned memory, as in study, or *memorizing*].

Memonemes: highly charged MIMPs, recording episodes from the past that were stressful or even overwhelming. Our term memoneme hearkens back to Ancient Greece: the goddess *Mnemosyne*, daughter of Uranus and Gaia (Heaven and Earth), was the mythological personification of memory. You meet her again in the English word mnemonic, an aid to memory.

Memonemes create unwanted emotions, distorted thinking and irrational behaviors.

The real violence and impact of these memonemes is the totality of what is wrong with Humankind and spirit destructive patterns. It is a paradox of considerable magnitude that the Being wanders through this and other universes, making recording of supposed happenings, and then uses them to hurt Self! It hardly makes sense.

Primaries. Memoneme primaries are the big deal. They bite and bite hard. Triggering a primary is capable of knocking a person flat. I have seen shrapnel drop out of a person's body, running a primary memoneme. I have seen individuals throw away their glasses or walking sticks. It's Lourdes stuff, without the religious cant.

Secondaries. These are still pretty tough but not as full-on as the primaries. Events of this nature would include dangerous illnesses, bereavements, divorce, bankruptcy, great public shaming and so on.

Tertiaries. These are the more everyday face of memonemes, the frequent and nuisance reminders of deeper events and structures, which keep us upset and create recurring unhappy feelings. Tertiaries can be getting in a rage with the wife, beating the kids, shouting at the boss and losing your job, or just getting aggressive in traffic.

Compare the definition of memonemes with *Samskaras*, a Hindu/Sanskrit word.

Threads

This reflects Freud's observation that episodes tend to run in a chronological sequence, first to last. Similar content seems to get joined up and becomes a chain or "thread", to use modern Internet jargon.

The Root

The first significant time something happened in a thread is its foundation event or "root". The plant metaphor is good, because it reminds us that when we rip out the root, the whole plant (the thread) will wither and die. Once we process the root and it loses its potency, the thread becomes harmless and is re-classified in the mind as "clean and useful memory", meaning it has learning value but no potential to cause harm.

Running (sometimes Rendering)

To run something means to go through it, in detail, experiencing it as the Now. The person gets immersed (see next definition). Something being "run" is the focus of attention. The pilot is addressing it; the client is processing it—looking at it form different angles

Immersion

This is a state of "time travel" in which the client goes back to a significant episode in memory and relives it, as if it were RIGHT NOW. He or she is "there". We want to hear descriptive phrases like: "I'm stepping through the doorway." Or, "He's hitting me in the face." And please not "I stepped through the doorway," or "Then he hit me in the face."

He or she may make movements that clearly come from the event, like jerking or writhing, saying the words again, out loud, or of course showing emotions like grief and anger.

Look and listen for these signs the person really is back there, sitting in the event. Being fully immersed is what makes the abreaction, or clean up process, work best.

Flattening

This means to keep at an item or memoneme, pounding it, running it and worrying it, until it finally has no more juice; it can no longer influence the person for ill; frankly, the client normally loses interest in an episode once flattened. It's gone; it's done. Safe!

Unburdening

Unburdening is what Hypnoetics™ is all about. It's a term from Freud (*Two Short Essays on Psychotherapy*). Freud showed us that releasing the emotional charge which comes from hidden elements of a thread will release the unpleasant emotional energy or "charge". This makes earlier instances come to light; a process he called unburdening.

Once unburdened of its charge and the root exposed, the whole thread collapses and loses its unpleasant impact: thoughts free up, emotions improve and behaviors start to make sense.

Re-Stimulation

Definition: to reactivate by stimulation (Merriam-Webster Online).

Semon told us that memory was not just about encoding recordings of what happened in life (or past incarnations, which he had never heard about); it's also about recovery of those memories when you need them. This process he called *ecphory*.

Obviously, we need to have both recording and recovery mechanisms, to get the effect we call remembering. But nobody had pointed this out till Semon's original insight.

I'm going to write about a special case of ecphory called restimulation. This is when the memory comes at you when you didn't need it or want it. Moreover, it brings with it unpleasant feelings, thoughts and behaviors.

The sequence is as follows:

Something unwelcome happens. A memory is recorded and is retained in the mind (not the brain, note). Usually, it gets buried but, like an antibody cascade: it is there and remembered, if the pathogen should return. Antibody manufacture can be resumed instantly. Memory can also be triggered instantly.

In the case of an unpleasant experience, when the same or similar circumstances manifest a second time, the original unpleasant memory is stirred up and comes back to life or is *re-stimulated*.

We usually feel bad (headache, irrational behavior, negative emotions—fear, unease, anxiety, etc.) without being aware of why we are upset. The underlying engram/memoneme remains hidden, buried subconsciously, exactly as Freud described (actually Janet).

The events of the second time do not need to be exactly identical to the original experience, just similar enough to trigger an association, leading to reactivation. Associations can be very loose, when things that are not identical are assumed to be identical; what Alfred Korzybski called "identification thinking" (a General Semantics term) or X=Y=Z, my joke.

In the previous chapter, I mentioned Semon's example of a dog, which sees a youth bending down to pick up something, followed shortly afterwards by an unpleasant pain, as the stone struck the dog. Ever afterwards, the dog is wary of people who bend down and one day, when someone bends over to tie his shoelaces, the dog feels the same pain, yelps in fright and runs away irrationally.

It's all logical, when you understand the context, which is the original memory. But the observed result is wholly unnatural and irrational seeming.

Semon tells us that this triggering, caused by the second stimulus, is at least in part an energetic response:

"On being subject again to this stimulus, or to other influences, the basis of which is invariably the partial recurrence of a definite energetic condition, the original state of excitement is reproduced" [*The Mneme*, my 1921 edition, p. 89]

Until the second event, nothing bad happens. We experience hurt at a specific time in a specific place; time moves on; we forget about it. It's just warehoused, not vanished. It remains latent, to use a scientific term. But then, one day: wham! Something brings it back to mind.

Trouble is, the restimulation experience is timeless. It can go on and on, repeating forever. One memory can lead to thousands of restimulation events. That's why these buried memories are so threatening and disturbing. It's like having a whip and scourging yourself with it from time to time... or for the rest of your life.

My good friend Prof. Clancy Mackenzie was on to this phenomenon, via a different route, and he called it the "two-trauma mechanism". You need a second occurrence or reminder, to kick a memoneme into action, whereupon it becomes a re-iteration, or new fractal copy.

Altered Behaviors

When something is restimulated, we tend to behave very differently. We experience the world differently and this is essential to grasp. If we were traumatized as a five-year old child, when encountering restimulation, we become a five-year old once again, in all but name.

We start reacting as the child would react; we feel what the child would have felt; we say what the child would have said at the time, in the child's voice. That's the enormously important thing about these restimulation moments: they shift us in time. They push us back down the timeline, to when it happened before.

Being out of time and place, of course, is just a kind of insanity. So thoughts and behaviors start to become very irrational.

Now at last you can understand why wonderful human beings—*the paragon of animals, noble in reason* (Hamlet)—will suddenly do something weird, strange, out of character. He or she has experienced the backward shift of a restimulation. He or she is out of present time. He or she is "living" the reactivated trauma.

We can use the term *dramatization* because the person is acting out their earlier role.

Anything Close Will Cause Restimulation

The big thing to grasp is that the second event need not be identical to the first but only approximately similar. So a child may get upset by the sight of a black hairbrush: why? Because it reminds him of the black moustache on the strange man who appeared when Mummy ran away and was never seen again. It can trigger a feeling of great loss and sadness.

Maybe as a man, this individual gets irritated every time he sees his wife brushing her hair with a black brush and is rude to her... but he can't explain it, or stop himself.

The first bereavement we experience in life may not be the worst emotionally. We may later experience a second bereavement which leverages on the first and becomes much more severe in impact.

It need not be so heavy. We can lose a sports game and feel, "I always lose. I'm no good" and go away upset. That was just a restimulation of earlier losses and failures.

These occurrences are just a variety of flashback but they can be very upsetting, while "hot" or active. Usually, the triggered emotional charge subsides rapidly. But not necessarily. Some people seem doomed to live in these unpleasant loops. They have no idea how to escape them.

So there are two more terms from Semon's book: *primary indifference* to an earlier unpleasant memory, meaning it just hasn't affected us yet, and *secondary indifference*, after the re-activation has died down. I'm not sure these terms serve much useful purpose. Both states we would describe as keyed out. But it's important to understand the latency of memonemes. They just sit there but can be re-activated any time. These are mental landmines; step on one and... Boom!

If a restimulation is shocking enough, a whole earlier memory may be charged up and become too overwhelmingly strong to easily shrug off. The memoneme is reactivated to the point of a full-on experience. We call this a *re-iteration*. When enduring and powerful enough, we can rightly use the term "delayed post-traumatic stress disorder".

Clancy Mackenzie MD made the concept famous in his book *Post-Traumatic Stress Disorders From Infancy*, written in conjunction with Lance Wright MD.

Delayed PTS Disorder

Very violent flashbacks are easily understood. They are sometimes the subject of movie stories.

A combat veteran exposed to loud bangs ten, twenty or thirty years after combat reacts in a predictable way. Flashes and people screaming will make it worse. Any event, sufficiently intense and sufficiently similar to earlier combat experience, can precipitate a flashback or even a delayed PTSD. The reaction is understandable because the initial combat experience was life-threatening.

But as Clancy Mackenzie points out, few realize that—to a baby—separation from the mother can be more frightening than war trauma to a soldier. For one hundred and fifty million years of patterning of mammalian behavior, separation from the mother has meant death, and thus the human infant is very sensitive and easily overwhelmed by events that would seem non-traumatic to the adult.

The fashionable term is an *attachment injury*; we come attached to someone and that attachment is threatened or broken. It can be a deep psychological wound.

This is the worst kind of re-iteration, which threatens to last for a lifetime. It is well-known, for example, that orphans and fostered children have huge psychological problems. Many are suffering from delayed post-traumatic stress disorder.

Clancy also became famous for proving the connection between delayed PTSD and schizophrenia. It figures.

Complex PTS Disorder

Now we have a new diagnosis called complex trauma disorder. *In a way, we all experience it, meaning life isn't that kind to any of us.* Pathological, never mind dysfunctional, parenting is almost universal today and can be very harmful and traumatic to the growing child.

Schooling, too, can be traumatic, with emotionally-inept teachers and peer bullying. I have said elsewhere that schooling can be the biggest wound we get in life, at least until later adulthood.

We grow up screwed up and then implant our issues in our kids, as a cultural "norm". It's what people do but, of course, common isn't the same as natural or healthy. Far from it.

Living in an intense and abusive relationship with someone can also constitute a complex trauma situation.

In an article called, "Understanding Complex Trauma, Complex Reactions, and Treatment Approaches" Dr. Christine Courtois summarizes complex trauma disorder as being subjected to stressors that are:

1. repetitive, prolonged, or cumulative

2. most often interpersonal, involving direct harm, exploitation, and maltreatment including neglect/abandonment/antipathy by primary caregivers or other ostensibly responsible adults, and...

3. often occur at developmentally vulnerable times in the victim's life, especially in early childhood or adolescence, but can also occur later in life and in conditions of vulnerability associated with disability/ disempowerment/dependency/age / infirmity, and so on.

One painful identification people make when they are victims of abuse occurs when they internalize their aggressor. In other words, they may start to identify with the person who hurt them the most, sometimes feeling protective or taking on their destructive point of view toward themselves.

All of us possess the critical inner voice (inner critic), but those who are traumatized may experience this "voice" as a deeply destructive and terrifying enemy, whose attacks can feel crippling and constant and can lead to life-threatening self-destructive behavior. When a person feels hopeless or isolated in their suffering or finds it difficult to trust easily, he or she can become further victimized by their critical inner voice, which denotes a state of chronic restimulation of the earlier trauma and delayed PTSD.

In turn, they may fail to have compassion for themselves and may make choices that repeat destructive patterns of their past. For instance, an abused child may wind up in an abusive relationship as an adult.

Universal Trauma Syndrome (UTS):

This is a Hypnoetics™ term, meaning continuous stirring of unpleasant memories triggered by our surroundings. The label simply reflects the fact that we are all affected, it happens a lot, and seems an almost inescapable aspect of human life. We are constantly being subjected to restimulators, causing endless re-iterations.

Hypnoetics™, and ultimately Supernoetics® advanced piloting (which you can learn about later), seem the best way to date to escape this endless jangle of our emotional nerves!

So far as had been determined to date, we are all under the sway of the same mechanisms of memory recording, charge and endless re-iteration of memonemes. To the degree we don't like re-experiencing bad stuff from the past, to that degree it is traumatic. Feeling bad is not natural to any of us (remember, common does not mean healthy).

A lot of modern psychological studies are expended on the investigation of supposed abnormal or pathological manifestations and functions. But this is naïve and assumes that people with the most disturbing and harrowing experiences are using their memory processes differently from the rest of us.

That's nonsense. The difference between someone with occasional or regular upsets and someone deeply wounded and permanently suffering from a stress disorder is only a difference in degree, not mechanism.

Memory Hijacking

As already explained, memory runs on automatic and has a retrieval system which is based, at least in part, on similarity of signals from the current environment to buried experiences of the past. That's useful for making rapid predictions about what is likely to happen in the immediate future.

In other words, that's a bit of lizard brain at work.

But it's not useful if the stored memory hijacks the entire process of computation. There has to be a useful similarity in comparing past to present circumstances. If it shifts to everything about the past equals everything about the future, we become useless; slaves of the overwhelming might of the former unpleasant experience, instead of active participants in our present-time environment.

It gets worse, however.

The experience of something like a re-iteration of a past unpleasant experience in present time forms a new layer at the tertiary level, which is now added in to the original memoneme structure.

In Semon's view, repetition of a stimulus does not strengthen an already existing [engram] memoneme, but generates a new memoneme (*The Mneme*, p. 169). However, Semon knew nothing of fractals.

When something is stirred up again, very similar in character to what has gone before, that's a mathematical property called "self-similarity" and it is a key characteristic of fractals. This has big implications...

The Fractal Nature Of Traumatic Memory ················

I believe Punk Psychology™ is the first writing to ascribe a fractal nature to traumatic memories and their repeated re-iterations. Buzz words like this get bandied around by people pretending credibility for their view of things (like the word "quantum"), so let's be clear about what a fractal really is...

The secret is the way the fractal is formed, which is that the output from a system or structure becomes the new input; that in turn is re-outputted and again, that's yet another new input. It goes round and around and around, evolving constantly, each new output becoming its own next input.

That means the growth of a fractal is very self-contained and self-regulated. Each iteration as it's called (repeat) pushes off in a slightly different direction but growth depends on what is already there. The beautiful pretty patterns we see are just a coincidence. The colors are artificial, added by writers of software code, to make the display look stunning.

The famous and beautiful Mandelbrot set, named after the late Harvard professor Benoit Mandelbrot, is based on the simple equation $Z = Z^2 + C$.

Each time you multiply out Z^2 and you add C, that becomes the new Z! The resulting fractal structure is just one among many.

In fact there are even deeper issues here: Mandelbrot created the first-ever "theory of roughness", as opposed to smooth and continuous, which is what normal experience tells us. Mandelbrot saw "roughness" in the shapes of mountains, coastlines and river basins; the structures of plants, blood vessels and lungs; the clustering of galaxies and many other places. His personal quest was to create some mathematical formula to measure the overall "roughness" of such objects in nature.

In Mandelbrot's own words:

The form of geometry I increasingly favored is the oldest, most concrete, and most inclusive, specifically empowered by the eye and helped by the hand and, today, also by the computer ... bringing an element of unity to the worlds of knowing and feeling ... and, unwittingly, as a bonus, for the purpose of creating beauty. [Mandelbrot, Benoit. *The Fractalist: Memoir of a Scientific Maverick*, Pantheon Books (2012)]

Fractals, not surprisingly then, are also found in many aspects of human creative activity, such as music, painting, architecture, heart rate variability, and even stock market prices.

Mandelbrot believed that fractals, far from being unnatural, were in many ways more intuitive and natural than the artificially smooth objects of traditional science and geometrical shapes.

To my knowledge, no-one before myself has ever connected structures of the mind and consciousness with "roughness". But then, Supernoetics® is right at the front end of noetic enquiries. You would hardly expect less from me!

Today the word fractal is often used to mean intricate folding and re-folding, weaving complex integrated patterns. We have "fractal antennas", for example, in our cell phones, to enable a large amount of transmitter and receiver function in a very compact space. These are very efficient aerials and the principle reason that cell phones will now fit comfortably in your hand.

In fact we are surrounded by fractals. They are core to the physical structure of our universe, which would make it hardly surprising if they are indeed a facet of consciousness!

Relating This to The eMind Sensor™

Where Semon's theories especially bear fruit is in relating them to important discoveries in electrophysiology. Continuing from the work of Carl Jung and later US chiropracter Volney Mathison, we have perfected the art of the electro-psychometer, that is: a sensitive biofeedback device that registers emotional and mental charges. Our particular version, the eMind Sensor™ (current model made by Ability Meters International), is one of the finest tools ever developed in this arena.

What we find happens is that a properly tuned psychometer can detect energetic changes related to mind activity. As Semon pointed out, the disturbance of memories and their re-activation is a true energetic phenomenon. It puts Punk Psychology™ in the field of advanced physics, not just psychobabble whimsy or behavioral doctrine (see also *Medicine Beyond* for the fuller physics story).

There are similarities with a lie detector, in that an electro-psychometer is basically a wheatstone bridge (compares resistances). But the idea it is a "lie detector" is nonsense. For one thing, you cannot detect lies, only stress. Secondly, it does not work on the principle of sweating, which is what today's pseudo-experts trumpet. The changes are much too fast.

We see needle movements that vary rapidly in both directions, even changes in speed of movement, in intervals down to as small as a fraction of a second. The idea one could sweat and then "unsweat" so rapidly is nonsense.

What really happens is that the psychometer responds to mental energies, especially emotions, and we can use this property to trace down threads or connections within the mind. This device has indeed been likened to a GPS for the mind.

It tells you where to look (geographically, so to speak), within the person's memory stacks.

We can also gauge an individual's mental "density", which we term the base reading. The higher the base, the denser the emotional energy cloud around a person.

Right away, we can tell when something is in restimulation and as the person talks about that particular body of charge (say a series of tertiaries), we can see the energy burning off and the impact lessening, as the memoneme is discharged.

Looking for active areas of charge, we follow a beat or "drop" to the right. The bigger the drop, the more the charge behind it.

We can call off a list of topics, or ask the client to talk, and then take up the subject with the biggest beat (drop). It doesn't mean it's the worst (most charged) thing that ever happened to the person, by any means. But it does mean the material is restimulated enough to be available to the conscious mind, with very little digging.

We know that at the bottom of that thread, far away and remotely buried, there lies a monster which sleeps. We don't disturb its tenebrous dreams...

What it amounts to is that we run lots of readily-confrontable items, to unburden the emotional reality of the present. We know these are easy to confront, because they read on the eMind Sensor™. Whatever reacts on the meter is just below the person's awareness; it's right there, sitting just under the surface and ready to process.

We can also relate case progress to the continuing rate of these beats or drops: as the needle continues to surge to the right, while the person talks and the unpleasant emotion is discharging, we can usually see the base reading fall steadily.

Essentially, what we are doing is restimulating charge in a controlled, manageable way, and deleting it permanently...Bring it into view, zap! Bring more into view, Zap! And so on...

The accumulated fall in base over the length of a breakout we call the "differential" and this will tell us that the client will feel good at the end. He or she will always use terms like "lighter" and "freer", as they experience the relief of dumping unwanted negative mental energies.

Most electro-psychometers today have automatic accumulators, to count the differential obtained in a breakout. Differential is measured in bars.

Layers Upon Layers ··

Using Hypnoetics™ we simply re-process experience, till it starts to make sense. The client sees things from a different perspective, feelings are mitigated, behaviors are modified. We knock the spots off troubled memory.

In time he or she comes to a shift, that massive process in which his or her whole worldview changes to something better, something more empowering, self-loving and true.

After sufficient recovery, the person is no longer connected to his or her basic memonemes. But he or she is still somewhat vulnerable. Think of it like defusing a bomb: the bomb is still there, all it needs it a new detonator and...!

We have to hurry to the next step, which is to release the force inherent in each memoneme. This in a way equates to soaking out the explosives with running water: it's no longer a bomb, just at empty hull where the TNT was once packed tightly.

OK, that's enough metaphors for this piece.

Let's go on now and apply what we've learned, *starting without the need for a GSR meter.*

Punk Points:

- Piloting means guiding, in the way a riverboat pilot steers the ship to a safe harbor. Pilots, in Hypnoetics™, are people trained to guide another person safely through their memory stacks (the hidden "library" of dark memories), all the while releasing negatively charged memories.

- Memories or MIMPS (short for mental image pictures or imprints) make up a continuous run of experience for an individual, from their first moment of awakening (even before birth), to the present. We call this string of MIMPs the person's timeline or, on a grander scale, the individual's world path (after Hermann Minkowski).

- The dark unpleasant MIMPs we call *memonemes*, which are of varying degrees of intensity and overwhelm. Later unpleasant experiences take almost all their power and force from earlier, buried, memonemes. Later iterations of these core memories we call restimulation and these have a fractal (self-similarity) character.

- We can address memonemes and reduce or eliminate their power over a person by bringing them fully into the light of day and getting rid of all adverse energy or "charge", a process we call flattening. The more fully flattened a memoneme, the more certainty that it cannot, any longer, adversely affect the individual concerned.

- The mechanism of continuously laying in charged memories, then stirring them around, triggering them over and over by hidden levers or reminders, is a process best termed "Universal Trauma Syndrome" (UTS). We all experience its unpleasantness to a degree. PTSD is just a severe and circumscribed version of UTS.

- Emotional or negative mental "charges" can be tracked using a simple feedback meter: the galvanic skin response or GSR meter. Such a device shows when charge is imminently rising to the surface, how it is being shed or released and, ultimately, that all such charge has dissipated—invariably accompanied by expressions of relief or even joy. It is not essential to use a GSR meter in Hypnoetics™. We can do a great deal of good without one.

CHAPTER 8

WHAT WE ARE DOING IN PILOTING

Let's look again at the phenomenon of post-hypnotic suggestion I described on page 87. It really is a crucial mechanism. At its most odious, this is a stage stunt by a sleazy, irresponsible con man (or woman).

Sometimes, what appears to be happening truly is. On other occasions it's merely an illusion. A trick.

But what people think they are observing goes somewhat as follows: the stage hypnotist (no hypnotherapist would do this in public) puts the volunteer into a trance. He (or she) then implants the idea that, "When I snap my fingers and you wake up, you will decide it is too warm in this room."

He snaps his fingers. The victim wakes up and takes off clothing, explaining they find the room unbearably warm. The audience roars with laughter. They know the secret. The poor victim doesn't understand the laughter and goes home upset. He or she may not sleep well for days, because the bedroom is "too warm".

What has happened here? An idea or fixed thought has been planted in the mind but is hidden from consciousness (the trance ensures that the memory is not processed by awareness in the normal way). So this buried thought or fixed idea is able to override reason and knowing.

We even have an expression indicating that some people are "more suggestible" than others. They pick up ideas and retain them, subconsciously, without seeming to have much resistance to the process.

But unscrupulous sales and media people actually pervert this tendency for their own gain, to control people by manipulating their mind content. Whenever you see an advertisement on TV portraying some warm, friendly, irresistible family scene, with gentle, reassuring music featured prominently and a strong emotional anchor (such as a cuddly child or pet animal), know that they are deliberately preparing the viewer for a post-hypnotic suggestion: go out and buy our product.

This dreamy-mood creation overrides the normal protective guards of the mind and allows content to enter that the person would not normally accept, without some form of compulsion. And commands are often given forcefully: call WXYZ number NOW, that's WXYZ... repeated over and over.

These advertisements are not an accident, or based on artistic design concepts; they are crafted carefully and cynically, with covert manipulation of the viewer's thoughts being the whole intent. This compulsion mechanism has been extensively researched for decades and can now be considered a fully-formed brain-washing technique.

So how does life do this to us? We don't go around listening to mushy music and looking at dreamy, out-of-focus images, do we!

The answer is duress. Stress. When overwhelmed, the mind's natural guard goes down and fixed ideas can enter, without much censorship. Say a woman is being assaulted or in fear of being raped. Her senses are heightened and her normal intelligent thinking processes are shut off. She's in survival mode. "Oh my God, men, they are animals, they want to do horrible things to you..." This is a fixed idea or "suggestion" that gets implanted. From then on, she has an aversion to men.

Trouble is, it's irrational. Like "the room is too warm" implant, she fears men even when there is no threat. According to the new mental programming, THAT man equals all men; all men are perverts and rapists; all men are dangerous. This becomes a hypnotic override that serves her very badly, simply because most men are not perverts and rapists, or even dangerous. It's a destructive lie entered into her case.

Definition: case. *It's the sum total of the person's non-optimum thoughts, disagreeable emotions and self-limiting behaviors.*

How do we deal with this? We cut out the lie. Like nifty surgery, we find out where the irrational thought came from, take off its force and violence, so she can examine it rationally and make a sensible decision about which men to trust and which ones to be careful of.

Of course not all life events are as extreme as rape and violence. But we pick up the same irrational conditionings that influence our response to other peoples (race, gender, age, sexuality and other issues), education, politics, social values, places and stages of our lives.

In short, we become the typical muddled, over-emotional, irrational, unhappy and overtly stressed human being. This state is so common it is considered "normal". I merely point out that normal does not mean the same as healthy or good; it just means widespread.

The Terrible Tiger Mechanisms

Now here's where it goes wrong. Many therapeutic approaches try to install yet another implant: "I'm OK. I'm safe from harm. I feel calm and centered around men..." This may be installed by repetition (affirmations) or by tapping energy points on the body; by chanting or dancing; by means of the therapist's authority; by reading self-help books; with prayers, ritual or belief; by taking happy pills; or any one of numerous other mechanisms.

They won't work. Nothing can be done here that is permanent. Why? Because the original implant is still installed. It hasn't gone away. It has claws and can still scratch when aroused [you can get rid of an unpleasant knocking sound from a car engine by using noise-cancelling headphones (try it!) but it will not save the engine from harm: the source of the knocking noise is untouched].

Think of this like a tiger sleeping, its head rested on its crossed paws. OK, it seems harmless enough... for the moment. But if something provokes the beast, it can unleash its terrible powers in an instant.

There are a number of unsatisfactory ways that individuals, knowingly or unknowingly, deal with the "sleeping tiger". One is to ignore it! Another is to step around it. Another is to stand still, paralyzed in fear, in case it should wake up. Run away is slightly more optimum than standing rooted to the spot. Attacking the tiger is another option but could get you badly hurt or maimed.

Learning to use the skills of animal trainer (piloting, we call it) would be the best and most assured way to deal with it. But to let it eat you alive is the worst of all (but commonest) response; in other words just succumb.

But the greatest of all is to LOVE that tiger! That's a whole new Punk Psychology™ strategy that others have not even considered over the millennia. It's beyond this piece but will appear in print soon.

In this context it is worth mentioning the old Zen metaphor of "riding the tiger back home". It's man and beast in affectionate accord. This means to have totally conquered one's case and inhibitions, to have mastered all fear and ignorance, to have discovered one's own magnificence and used the power of knowledge to transform the experience of Being into a final show of light and wisdom!

[Do not confuse this metaphor with that of "having a tiger by the tail" or the Chinese, being "unable to get off" the back of a tiger].

The Process

The way we uninstall these dysfunctional implants is easy in principle. The secret is to locate, accurately, where they are buried in the mind. There is an exact date and location. We use the term "piloting" to denote this guidance process.

It helps also to have a reliable map and GPS device, so you don't get lost! We have those too. But using a GSR meter is not essential, proving you keep to the proper paths and follow instructions carefully.

Once found and fully exposed, these negative implants (we use a technical term memonemes, meaning harmfully charged memories (named for the Greek goddess of memory Mnemosyne), will quickly dissolve.

It is not quite so simple, in the sense that many of these charged memories get interlocked. Memonemes are strung together in "threads" and we need to pull out the core event, or "root". Freud taught us that principle, which he called unburdening.

Eradicating a memoneme is just the reverse of fractal growth: stripping off the layers, like peeling an onion, by simple repetition. It pares memory back to the truth. There is now scientific validation of this process, as we will see later.

The point being that sooner or later (usually sooner) the individual realizes the true origin of their distraction, issue or irrationality and the whole thing satisfyingly vanishes.

It's like clearing weeds (sorry, another metaphor): we pull them up, one by one and the flowers can then flourish. We have a term "negative gain", meaning getting better by getting rid of stuff. The vanishment is often so complete, the individual no longer even remembers having the problem! It takes a friend to remark, "Say, you don't seem to have much of a fear of dogs any more!" for the person to realize there has been an improvement.

The reason for that is simple: happiness, abundance, wisdom, strength and love are our natural states of Being. So removing the clutter simply allows these beautiful flowers to unfold from within us. The experiences we had don't erase. But we are freed of their impact on our basic thought processes. We become "more me", which after all is what the term Supernoetics® means (super- more or better; noetics, mind and spirit).

Reference Memories

One of the important Punk Psychology™ mechanisms is the establishment of "reference memories". This needs careful explanation.

When you have thoroughly cleaned up a subject or episode, the client feels differently about it. The "new" memory you created, using the MINT technique, becomes the future reference memory, or goto memory, if you like. The client no longer plunges for the pain and disempowerment.

So if a person's sister died tragically in a motor accident, the moving on, stepping free, laying-the-past-to-rest memory you created for him or her will become the reference memory from now on. This is an important contribution we have made to personal empowerment and freedom.

If a person has "dealt" with a subject from the past but it was not with our Hypnoetics™ PP approach, or the more advanced 4-tier technique (4TT) developed by Heidrun Beer and Rolf Dane, you may be sure it will still be very much "alive" at some deeper level. The memoneme the client carries is still the reference datum. He or she is just tippy-toeing around it (see the Terrible Tiger mechanisms, page 105).

How do I know the charge is still there? It's not a rule; but I have never met anyone who had used faith healing, EFT, hypnotism, EMDR, Sedona, meditation, etc. to "deal with" an unpleasant event, who didn't immediately starts bawling when I sent them back to it, making it NOW.

We can do this quite ethically, because we need to know. It's a really foolish mistake to leave past charge unaddressed because the client says, "it's gone". If you are the chosen helper, you are quite entitled to say, "Well, let's just travel back there, in your mind's eye, and see if anything got missed or left incomplete..."

Get the date and location and MINT it.

But don't be surprised if the sensate awareness explodes right in front of you! Writhing, tears, angry words, whatever. Just deal with it properly this time, for pity's sake!

Harmonizing Mind and Body

Scientists think the mind is in the brain. We say: the brain is in the mind, or the body is in the mind. Memory lives a great deal in the body. This is something you will discover in piloting.

Past trauma draws your attention units in a very powerful way. Half or more of your mind and Being may be focused on earlier trauma and abuse, meaning you are far from fully alive in the present.

It's easy to say, "Get a grip" and take your mind off events that are long past. But it's all-but impossible, if you don't have the tools of Punk Psychology™ (Hypnoetics™) and advanced Supernoetics® to help you.

A brilliant book *The Body Keeps the Score* by Bessel van der Kolk, professor of psychiatry at Boston University School of Medicine, sheds new light on just how disastrous mental trauma can be, taking its toll on the health of the physical body.

But how deep does it go? In my writings, I have been saying for over twenty years that trauma memories live IN the body. Forget the brain. The body holds most of our trauma memories—and I don't mean physical trauma, I mean mental trauma.

The trauma caused by childhood neglect, sexual or domestic abuse and war wreaks havoc in our bodies, says professor van der Kolk. Trauma and its resulting stress harms us through physiological changes to body and brain, and that those harms can persist throughout life. Excess stress can predispose us to everything from diabetes to heart disease, maybe even cancer.

Van der Kolk draws on 30 years of experience to argue powerfully that trauma is one of the West's most urgent public health issues. The list of its effects is long: on mental and physical health, employment, education, crime, relationships, domestic or family abuse, alcoholism, drug addiction. "We all want to live in a world that is safe, manageable... predictable, and victims remind us that this is not always the case," says van der Kolk. When no one wants to hear about a person's trauma, nothing gets resolved. And the result is it finds a way to manifest in their body.

Well, we can resolve things very capably, with Punk Psychology™.

Remember, it is not only extreme experiences that linger. Family disturbance or generalized neglect can wire children to be on high alert, their stressed bodies tuned to fight or flight. Or they may be so "numbed out" by keeping demons at bay they can't engage with life's pleasures or protect themselves from future trauma.

Even parents who just don't attune with their children can do untold damage, van der Kolk argues. Neglect creates mental maps used by children, and their adult selves, to survive. These maps skew their view of themselves and the world.

The book has gut-wrenching stories: about Vietnam veterans who committed war atrocities, incest survivors, broken adults that were terrorized as children or shunted between foster homes. Van der Kolk draws on hundreds of studies to back up his claim that "the body keeps the score".

More to the point, our minds hold the memonemes of disaster very close. Only we can release them fully and forever It's like shedding chains and shackles for many.

We Can Go Further

This story gets richer, by far.

Once we have worked on case for a while (100 to 200 hours, typically), we start encountering real magic. The person begins to develop marvelous powers of psychic perception. Out-of-body states are common. Prescience and remote viewing no longer seem strange or impossible. Telepathic experiences become commonplace. Probable past lives swim into view.

We are no longer just "creature".

It's an extension of negative gain, meaning that as worldly strife and pain are obliterated from memory, our true spiritual abilities begin to blossom too. We are non-material conscious beings, a state called theta. We can get back to that state, without mischief or strange practices. It's natural. For over forty years I have seen people emerge from their cocoon of suffering and despair, to discover the freedom of the cosmos; to live, Be, experience and explore the total universe in which we find ourselves (there seem to be multiple other universes but that's another story).

Now let me tell you another hypnotism case; this one far different from the first. When the limitations of the mind are transcended, nothing seems impossible. We truly pass beyond the so-called "laws" of physics.

Michael Talbot tells the story in his blockbuster book *The Holographic Universe*. A hypnotist had been hired to entertain family and friends. There were the usual stage tricks. But the amazing event was the moment one of the guests, Tom, was hypnotized and told that when he came out the trance, his daughter Laura would be totally invisible.

Then, after having Laura stand directly in front of the chair in which Tom was sitting, the hypnotist awakened him and asked him if he could see her and the answer was "No". Laura just giggled. Nothing special so far, just mind stuff.

But then the hypnotist went behind Laura so he was hidden from Tom's view and pulled an object out of his pocket. He kept the object carefully concealed so that no one in the room could see it, let alone Tom, and pressed it against the small of Laura's back. He asked Tom to identify the object. Tom leaned forward as if staring directly through Laura's stomach and said that it was a watch. The hypnotist nodded and asked if Tom could read the watch's inscription. Tom squinted as if struggling to make out the writing and recited both the name of the watch's owner (which happened to be a person unknown to anyone in the room) and the message.

The hypnotist then revealed that the object was indeed a watch and passed it around the room so that everyone could see that its inscription was exactly as Tom had discerned through his daughter's flesh and blood. She was indeed transparent.

Afterwards Tom confirmed that his daughter had been absolutely invisible to him. All he had seen was the hypnotist standing and holding a watch cupped in the palm of his hand. Had the hypnotist let him leave without telling him what was going on, Tom would never have known he wasn't perceiving normal reality.

The point I am making is that these abilities are real. Tom was in no way unique. We can all do it, once we rid ourselves of limitations.

If these manifestations fascinate you and seem to be calling, then Supernoetics® is your path. We are already far ahead with our researches into this kind of transcendent phenomenon. But we don't use hypnotism; we use your own abilities, powers that are hidden deep within you. Since you were a child you have been told repeatedly you cannot have such abilities. And so you have lost them.

Backwards and Forwards In Time

As I said, the main technique of Hypnoetics™ is about controlling and maneuvering the client's timeline. If you can do that confidently, you're more than halfway there.

The best analogy for this is to think of a VCR tape and liken it to using the rewind, stop, PLAY and fast-forward buttons. You say to the client: "Go to the time you were standing on Brooklyn Bridge." You expect him or her to do just that. Said with enough authority in your voice, and the client relaxed and fully attentive, he or she will have very little choice.

It's like asking him or her to "Rewind the tape to the point where you were standing on Brooklyn Bridge." The tape is the timeline, of course.

When you want the client to work through the episode or event, you say "Move through this event to a point six weeks later," and he or she should understand you are saying hit the PLAY button and let the recording roll forward to a time six weeks after you were standing on the Brooklyn Bridge. No further.

If the client doesn't get it quickly, use this analogy and re-train him or her to listen to your commands and do just what you are asking.

You could also take a sheet of paper and mark a timeline along the long side, put some dates on it, and then slide it backwards and forwards in mimicry of the movements of attention. Put a pen down opposite the paper, to represent the person's attention focus; slide the dates past it, backwards and forwards, till he or she gets the idea. From then on, it's easy!

The Two Types Of Recall

There are really two ways people recall things. The difference is crucial.

1) Memory straightline: the patient stays in the here-and-now and simply throws a line back to the past and hauls in the memory, like casting a fishing line and hauling in the fish. It has its uses. It's how we learn at school, for instance. But it's not therapeutic.

2)   Reliving, as now: the patient goes back to the time and re-experiences it, re-lives it in fact, as if it was the now. You want to hear descriptions like, "I am opening the door, I walk into the room and there she is..."

The former does not engage the client, the latter fully engages him or her. No trance is needed for reliving, but the person has to be down there, in the past, recounting and reliving everything that happens.

You'll know, because there will be emotion, pain, sighing, tears, discomfort, words spoken and thoughts of the moment being voiced. You will actually SEE the person re-experiencing the memory. He or she is right there, living it, not just "remembering" it.

There is in fact a third type of recall, in which the client views events from a distance, looking down on it and feeling detached. We call this the glass elevator view. This does have some healing potential, and we employ it when a person is really sucked in and suffering heavily from heavy pains or emotions that have been turned on and are not easy to endure (see remedies in chapter 13).

Punk Points

We are nowhere near hypnotizing the client or getting an effect by implanting positive ideas. We are UN-hypnotizing people from experiences on the timeline; notably the unpleasant happenings of the past and the accompanying pain.

The mind is very powerful in imposing its agenda on consciousness. It may be impossible for the individual to see where problems and "case" are coming from. We lead them to the source, which is why we call it piloting (steering).

When there's a difficulty or a horrendous experience in our past, there are several ways the person deals with his. We call these The Terrible Tiger Mechanisms: avoidance, ignore it, stepping past it, being paralyzed and unable to respond at all, or maybe (crazy) attacking the tiger! We can add learning animal-taming skills, which is what Punk Psychology™ really is. That way we can manage the tiger.

Loving the tiger is the ultimate path to love, freedom and release. But that requires skills you may not have yet. You get them from studying Supernoetics®, as well as just Punk Psychology™!

A key concept for what we can achieve is that of reference memories. These are what the client responds to reflexly in any given situation. But when we pilot skillfully, properly cleaning up the charge and irrationality, the person comes to a new view (shift). He or she now has a new goto or "reference memory", which is what automatically comes to mind for that particular person or topic.

CHAPTER 9

UNIVERSAL TRAUMA SYNDROME

In an earlier chapter I introduced new ideas about *delayed* post-traumatic stress disorder and also what is commonly known as complex trauma syndrome. I hinted that we all suffer from something of the kind and, in fact, in Hypnoetics™ (and the mother subject of Supernoetics®) we recognize the condition of Universal Trauma Syndrome, or UTS. Universal because it's everywhere; no-one is exempt.

Modern psychologists are studying such effects for all they are worth. But they work almost exclusively with sick or troubled people, with stories of abuse, addiction, phobias and insanity. They understandably lose sight of the fact that the same mechanisms are at work in us all.

Researches have shown that psychic trauma everywhere abounds, is held within us, is capable of causing immense damage to emotional and physical health, and is generally badly understood and not well dealt with. In other words, *we all suffer from stress* but in varying degrees.

Hidden emotional charge from psychic events of the past is real, buried (sometimes very deeply) and extremely damaging.

The Hardy Personality ··

The thing is, each of us has different tolerance to stress and trauma events. What is miserable adversity to one may be a stimulating "challenge" for another. The same setback, such as a divorce or bankruptcy will have different effects on each individual, according to how well they cope. This is partly a function of concomitant load factors, as explained above. But also in part a measure of each person's inner resistance or vitality.

In other words stress is not an event, as such, but *how you perceive that event.*

One can conceive, as Chicago psychologist Suzanne Kobasa does, of the "hardy personality". She came up with this theory while studying stressed executives and noticed that while half fell ill to stress-related diseases, the other half remained fit and cheerful.

She identified the main characteristics of the survivors by three "C"s:

- Commitment - to themselves, their family and their job
- Control - being able to make changes; not being helpless
- Challenge - the determination that life's switches and tumbles were part of the thrill of being alive.

Elsewhere in Supernoetics® we talk about the life effects scale (FX plot) and it is our view that those riding high on the curve, who are filled with zest, happiness and vitality, are immeasurably more able to cope with disaster than those who are running low on life energy. True, a big setback will bring even the hardiest type downwards on the graph. But the whole point is the higher you start out, the more reserve you have; the further it is to hit rock bottom.

It's a kind of safety margin between you and failure or death.

The fact is that buried mental traumas don't just vanish. They can be ignored, worked around or denied, but they don't go away. Years of research into cases, who have been worked up with emotional freedom technique, Sedona, counseling, etc. and yet still, *when you ask the right question in the right way*, dissolve into a morass of tears... it was not eradicated. There was only the pretense of a solution. The person is still oppressed by their past traumas.

It affects everyone; hence our term: universal trauma syndrome or UTS. Let's dig a little deeper, starting with the concept of "stress". It's a word we all use, yet with little real understanding of what it means, beyond feeling unpleasant.

Stress is one of the commonest reasons for consulting a doctor, second only to coughs and colds. Ironically, the medical profession has little to offer, beyond tranquillizing drugs and bland advice.

Yet stress is something uniquely personal, which we alone are really able to control for ourselves. First it is necessary to understand what stress is and then, if you cannot altogether remove it, you need strategies for counterbalancing its dangerous effects. Because make no mistake, stress *in its fullest sense* is the world's number one killer.

What we know today is that stress, or shall we broaden it to the term psychic trauma, will visit into your physical body.

What Is Stress?

So what is stress? Fundamentally, it is any threat or counter-pressure on your survival; in other words anything which limits or opposes your life potential. This can mean fear of losing a loved one, money worries or anxiety when flying. Stress truly has many faces.

In biological terms, this can be compared to the classic "fight or flight" situation. There is a threat and certain over-drive mechanisms are brought into play, ready for the encounter. Most noteworthy is the familiar adrenalin reaction, which increases heart rate and blood pressure. But there are many other changes that the body makes in preparation for extreme effort, such as mobilization of steroid hormones, increased perspiration, faster breathing, the liver breaks down fats for energy, digestion stops and saliva dries up. While transient, there is little problem.

But when the tension is continued too long, it can become damaging to have the body continue in this hyper-alert condition.

In this event, numerous symptoms develop, such as depression or anxiety, aches and pains, loss of appetite and insomnia. The individual is likely to become extremely irritable and difficult to live with. This deterioration in interpersonal levels is one of the saddest and most damaging aspects of our modern stressful way of life.

Unhappiness and the downgrading of love and affection is a tremendous price to pay for living in the fast lane or keeping up with the metaphorical Joneses.

Other Forms Of Stress

It is not widely understood that there are many forms of stress, over and above the classic mental pressures such as money worries, failed relationships and bereavements.

Dysfunctional sleep patterns stress the body. So does poor diet, chemical pollution and working too hard. Inadequate nutrition is one of the biggest causes of biological stress. Some foods are worse than others and we can introduce the term "stressor foods".

Viral and other illnesses are also stresses on the body, though it must be remembered that it becomes a circular jeopardy, because stress causes illness, which causes more stress, and so on.

There are many other less obvious alarms, such as the constant background threat of nuclear annihilation or ecological nemesis and the accelerating pace of history. We cannot escape these fears, whether consciously or subconsciously. Those who appear not to care are merely suppressing the danger within and that in many ways is even more dangerous than confronting it.

Finally, if that were not enough, we have technological advances that are now so complex and rapid there is a real danger of physical meaning to the metaphorical term "mind-blowing".

Overload

What all this adds up to is the increasing likelihood of overload. Our biological defence systems can cope admirably well, *but there is a limit*. We are just expecting too much of our biological machines, which after all take millions of years to evolve new stratagems and forms.

When there is just too much to keep abreast with, we enter the state of overload and things start to go wrong, a little at first but then with rapidly advancing deterioration in our physical condition. What begins as just a few attacks of indigestion can soon become a stomach ulcer, then cancer and then death, all within a few years of the first signals.

Important: What is not appreciated is that by the time symptoms begin to appear it is *too late*. The very emergence of signs of damage (which is what symptoms are), means that the defence mechanisms have begun to break down. *They can no longer protect you.*

By the time you *feel* ill, your body has probably been suffering damage for many years. The body has cleverly compensated. But when this protection runs out, like bad spending, your account is bankrupt and you are in dead trouble.

The onset of illness is often a complex process. The causes can appear misleading to the careless or ignorant observer. You may have been having a bad diet for many years, too much alcohol, lack of sleep and lack of restorative exercise. Then someone dies and you fall ill. "Ah, stress related due to bereavement", someone says.

But the bereavement may simply, as in this case, be the last straw. There were many other hidden factors at work and the loss of a loved one was simply the trigger factor. Given a good diet, exercise and even a little self-care, this individual would not have fallen ill, merely grieved a little and then moved on.

It is *wrong* to blame just one factor when illness manifests. It is always a summation of complex interactions, each of which contributes something to the damage. I call this a cascade effect.

The Signs Of Overload

Factually, the symptoms of too much stress are almost infinite. There are few specific symptoms. Generally, what the individual experiences is symptoms related to what we call "end-organ failure". When overload has gone onto to breaking point, the weakest part of the body will snap first. This is where the earliest symptoms appear.

If the digestive system is weakest, there will be indigestion and other disturbance, maybe ulcer, colitis and eventually bowel cancer. If the circulation is weakest, there will be blood pressure or heart attack. Symptoms referred to the lungs include asthma, cough or shortness of breath. Endocrine gland breakdown can cause diabetes, thyroid problems, adrenal stress and so on.

When the brain is affected, symptoms can be very diverse because this is where all our experiences meet. Apart from the obvious symptoms, such as anxiety and depression, there can be many strange subjective feelings (subjective means only the person in question feels them), like "seeing myself in the distance, down a long tunnel," or "like ice cold water running down my back and legs".

None of these descriptions will sound familiar to the doctor and therefore the patient is likely to be dismissed as a crank, or worse!

Finally, of course, women have their own troubles and PMT (PMS) or the monthly blues are just one example of what happens when the system starts to malfunction.

How Much Is Too Much?

One of the problems in studying stress is to determine its onset. What can seem a mildly stimulating and even entertaining challenge to one person can seem like the end of the world to another who cannot cope sufficiently and collapses under the strain.

In other words stress is very subjective. Indeed, the overload concept will tell us right away that what is stress on one occasion when the load is high may not cause any reaction another time, when the other load factors are eliminated.

Probably the most famous analysis of the health consequences of stress is the so-called Holmes-Rahe Social Readjustment Rating Scale. Thomas H. Holmes and Richard H Rahe of the University of Washington School of Medicine interviewed over 5,000 cases and showed that the more stress you experienced, the more likely it was that you would suffer some kind of health breakdown in the subsequent 2 years.

They went further and were able to produce a league table of disaster, which rated each life event according to severity and likeliness of ill-health. The top 3 events concern break up of longstanding relationships, whether by death or divorce and this will come as no surprise to those who have had to endure such suffering. Also appearing are marriage, change of job, jail term, pregnancy and large mortgage. It is interesting to note that even what are supposed to be pleasing life events, nevertheless carry their stress toll (marriage, birth and getting a raise).

The New Rating On The Holmes And Rahe Scale ·······

A new scale of rankings were drawn up in 1997 by psychiatrists from the Veterans Affairs Medical Centre in Reno, Nevada, based on a study of 427 volunteers who were asked to assess 87 life events.

The study was published in the *Journal of Psychosomatic Research* and reported by Hospital Doctor. Women scored 86 of the 87 events as more stressful men. But, so the explanation goes, it is not women who are over-reacting but men who are under-reacting!

It was reckoned that stress, overall, has increased by 45% in the 40-year period since Holmes and Rahe carried out the first study.

Unmarried people gave higher scores across the range of events. It suggests that being married or attached is a far safer way to face life's trials and that you will live longer and be more healthy if you are married. This has been shown before to be a true medical fact.

The old and new scales are as follows:

1997.

1. Death of spouse

2. Divorce

3. Death of close family member

4. Marital separation

5. Fired from work

6. Major illness or injury

7. Jail term

8. Death of close friend

9. Pregnancy

10. Major business readjustment

11. Loan repayment demand

12. Gain new family member

13. Marital reconciliation

14. Change in health of family member

15. Change in financial state

1977.

1. Death of spouse

2. Death of close family member

3. Fired from work

4. Divorce

5. Pregnancy

6. Jail term

7. Loan repayment demand

8. Marital separation

9. Change in health of family member

10. Marriage

11. Retirement

12. Sexual difficulties

13. Change in financial state

14. Gain new family member

15. Death of close friend

A Brilliant Definition Of Stress

Exclusively for Punk Psychology™, I have developed a masterful and unique definition of stress: *stress is the difference between what you have got and what you wanted!*

Think about this. The further apart the two scenarios are, the most you need to change to get to where you want to be; the more mental tension; the bigger the disappointment if you fail.

So a man who wants to be rich and is stony broke is going to feel worse about it than a happy-go-lucky guy who never worries about money! A woman who wanted to marry a nice, loving, safe man is going to feel far worse if she finds she has married a brute than she would if her husband was merely incompetent.

Stress is measured by the size of the gap. If what you have got is exactly what you wanted, then there is no stress at all. Do you see?

This does not invalidate or overwrite any other workable definition of stress. It's brilliant in that it works alongside any other model.

So - What Can You Do?

There are a number of ways to enter the field of stress reduction. It is a question of reducing the overload and it can be tackled at several points.

You may be going through a bankruptcy or divorce. These are extremely difficult times and it is somewhat naive to suggest you act in a laid back fashion. More sensible would be to deal with the things that you *can* control, such as leisure, diet and a reduced workload. Try to ease the other aspects of your life until the main aggravation is ended.

The general principle is to improve things along several fronts at once, rather than picking a fad and being fanatical about that one aspect of health. It is little use taking up daily jogging to improve your health, for example, if you make no effort to change your diet or establish more control over your work environment. You are unlikely to live longer.

Indeed you may well be one of the unlucky few who drop dead of worry and work overload while on a jogging and fitness program!

Most important of all - and this is the doctor talking to you - is *love*. You need to be anchored by a loving and nourishing relationship through these stressful times. If someone is standing beside you, sharing the knocks (and the triumphs too!), there is no doubt that you will ride over disaster with fewer wounds and hurt.

This cuts both ways: you may be going through a very bad time, coping with immense stress. *Under no circumstances take it out on your lover or family*. It is tempting to do so but this is the high road to a wrecked home. You need them as surely as they need you. If times are tough *double your output of love*. Others around you will respond as surely as if you had infected them with a plague!

The final answer to stress - all stress, all categories and all degrees - is *love*.

L-O-V-E.

And Hypnoetics™ piloting, of course! OK, upwards and onwards...

Punk Points: ···

- There is no universal definition of stress; it means different things to different people. But there is no question that *what the individual perceives as stress is damaging, both mentally and physically* to him or her.

- Holmes and Rahe gave a quantified tabulation of different stresses in a person's life. They found even supposedly-pleasant events, like getting married or getting a raise, could be stressful.

- As well as classic mental pressures such as money worries, failed relationships and bereavements, stress can also come from lack of sleep, poor diet, chemical pollution, a viral illness, working too hard and wrong foods.

- In Hypnoetics™ we have developed a masterful and unique definition of stress: *stress is the difference between what you have got and what you wanted!*

CHAPTER 10

MANAGING THE TIMELINE

Hypnoetics™ has best been described as manipulating a person's timeline. That's all we really do! We send the client back to a significant moment, he or she really travels back in time, bringing the memory back to life, as if it was NOW. We then shunt him or her back and forth through the episode, each time newly, until all the charge, wretched thoughts, emotions, pain and confusion all come off.

Sure, you'll see some tears. It's a good sign, meaning the person is fully engaged or "immersed" as we term it. You may see physiological changes, like turning red in the face (or pale), sweating, shivering or trembling, grimaces or shifts in posture. But don't worry, it comes out alright in the end, provided you keep going.

Think of it like replaying a VCR tape recording of the episode under scrutiny; you hit the rewind, to get to the beginning, then press PLAY and step back. As the MIMP fully plays out, there is a wholesale repeat of the original drama: the original thoughts, feelings, movements, words, posture, and so on.

The official term for this process of waking up memories—bringing them back to life—is called reconsolidation (see below).

When it's played through, you hit rewind and then hit PLAY again. And again and again.

It's hard at first for the beginner pilot to believe that he or she is controlling another person's timeline in this way but you do. All it takes is firmness. Say, "Move to July 1967" in the business-like way a conductor would call out, "Pass right down the car, please," and the person's timeline will slide past in front of you. Without being able to help themselves, clients will go back to the point you just designated.

If it doesn't lift nicely in this way, with obvious relief and a cheery smile, we ask for something earlier on the thread: *is there an earlier related episode/memory?* That's a workhorse phrase. Memorize it.

We may also use: *Are there earlier experiences like this?* or *Can you find something more fundamental?* The important point is that there really is no right or wrong, providing you understand what we are looking for.

Sometimes, by going earlier, we go all the way down to the root. Other times the client has a magical awakening with a significant shift in viewpoint, and we leave off, at least for the time being.

Time Tools

So if we are moving a person around on the timeline, we need to have a method for setting a date. We find there are four main ways to pinpoint time:

- Numbers: 18 years, September 1976, 99 million years ago.

- Place: The time you were in Rome, a week after you moved to Dallas, the moment you were standing together on Brooklyn Bridge... and so on.

- Occasion: the time you passed your driving test, just after the divorce, on the eve of your fifteenth birthday...

- Significance: the time you first realized he didn't love you, when you found yourself scared, when you realized for the first time that you were totally alone...

Any of these variants, used boldly, will send the person immediately to that location on their timeline. He or she can't resist, if you are in control and express your authority in your voice.

Not Psychoanalysis

This is NOT psychoanalysis, counseling, life coaching or similar. We don't discuss things. We are not interested much in the client giving interpretations they have been served up ("I think this is just a coping mechanism really..."). Certainly, the pilot is forbidden to give any suggestions or interpretations (see chapter 13).

Get it (reconsolidate), drop the person back there, run it, run it again, and again and again, using different sense modalities. Is all!

Just narrative, in other words. If the client starts on endless "explanations" of this sort, gently put a stop to it and say, "Tell me what is actually happening... thank you."

Pilots could not give a hoot about what earlier, incompetent therapists have laid on the case. We just want to know what happened, exactly, what feelings and sensations were felt, who was there, what was said, the sequence of movements, the impact of energy, etc. Time, place, who is there, what is taking place.

For someone who has spent years getting screwed up by "therapists" in this way, they may assume you want to do the same. Gently disabuse him or her and point out the differences in procedure. It's running through an episode, not talking about thoughts. We don't do "explanations", just discharge things. If it doesn't discharge, we are not being effective.

Of course we do not refuse marvelous realizations that frees up the person's thinking. Those "Aha!" moments are what we strive for (see Cognosis section below).

Later I'll teach you how to observe signs that all is going well, even without a GSR meter.

Go Earlier

Freud taught us long ago that if something doesn't discharge and release pretty quickly, there is earlier related material. We think in sequences of similar episodes called threads. They track back to a formative episode that we call the root. Pull up the root and the plant (thread) dies.

There may not be an earlier event but may be an *earlier beginning* to the episode you are working on. For example, the client is running a bereavement and he/she realizes that it started as an unhappy occasion when the first symptoms of cancer appeared, not just at the time of bereavement. Or a person relates a break up with their significant other... but then realizes it began months or even years before with a particular realization that all was not well. From then on it was relentlessly downhill, *leading* to the break up.

You may even find with some cases that they can psychically "feel" when something is coming on and—for him or her—it starts there, rather than with the beginning of the real world process loop.

However, be sure not to abandon running an episode that is running well, changing structure rapidly and, if you are using biofeedback, giving loads of meter action. You would be better to work the sensate awareness out of an episode with good meter action, rather than leave it in search of something else.

It won't hurt to ask for something earlier; if he or she says there is nothing, just continue running the episode you are on.

Dramatizing

One thing you will soon learn is the spectacle we call "dramatizing" (acting out). In this state the client appears to have truly become someone from the past. You can see a face change utterly, in Jekyll and Hyde fashion, and at times the shouting (screaming even), calls for help and other invective can become truly piteous.

His or her voice may change completely. There have been many instances of someone speaking in a different language or "speaking in tongues". The person seems to have become someone else and, in fact, very probably has become another identity, for the time being.

It's not common but I have seen a client literally picked up and shaken with extreme force, once they get into a heavily-charged event. Sometimes you worry that the yells can be heard down the block and the police will be called, because obviously someone in the room is being tortured or murdered (often that's true if you are running a buried past life death). No matter; he or she will have calmed down by the time the cops arrive!

We just let all this roll over us, realizing that the person is acting out something deep in memory. It's like playing a part in a violent movie. The Structures of Communication Clinical Workshop training we offer helps prepare and train us for such moments, teaching us to be calm, in control and exterior to the fuss.

The answer to getting past these moments of extreme turmoil are to be simply confident, maintain control, and give the next required command. Don't panic and don't quail. As the charge releases, he or she will soon calm down.

At times like these, simply remember Robert Frost's beautiful admonition: *the best way out is the way through* (from the poem, *A Servant To Servants*). Just push him or her onwards. It will all soon resolve.

Awesome

Once you have been witness to this awesome power of the mind, you will never doubt again that it is capable of utterly ruining a person's life and wrecking health. You will also be vividly aware of the power, the force, wrapped up in a single memory.

The timeline is very scary at times, brutal even.

Mostly, however, it's fun and fascination. We can handle it safely and smoothly. When someone gets stirred up remember: it wasn't you that did it. The person's own mind is the source of the turmoil. You only tripped the reaction. That's not a wicked thing to do. People cannot protect themselves from their own past by living in denial; it does nothing to resolve a case.

It takes courage to face the past and I respect that. It also takes courage to take someone by the hand, step into the lion's jaws and come out with a happy result. I especially admire my pilots, for that reason. We can fix things and we can change lives so much for the better.

We can change the world, one MIMP at a time (well, whole bunches at once but you know what I mean)!

It can't be exaggerated or overstated that memonemes are the core of human irrationality and misery... We want them disabled or, more exactly, brought to reason.

Landmines

I want you to think of what we do as detonating the landmines in a person's past. We need to really explode them... Bang! That way they are rendered harmless and can never come back to hurt the person.

This is the core difference between what we do in piloting and what other fashionable therapies do. We are NOT papering over the cracks, "coming to terms with", rationalizing, justifying, releasing, or any other variant of coping or managing.

We want the charge OUT, gone, the memoneme permanently transformed into a clean, useful memory that cannot bother the client ever again. Savvy?

This Is More Scientific Than You Think!

I first taught this method over a quarter of a century ago, knowing full well it worked beautifully.

I was surprised and gladdened therefore to see that science has backed up the Hypnoetics™ method. Punk Psychology™ meets punk science!

Completely new memory research is showing us that when memories are re-activated, they are in some way vulnerable to being changed. In fact decisive steps at that time can disengage the "maladapative behavior" associated with the memory (maldapative just means "not doing you any good"!)

"The theoretical argument is that when you initially present stimuli, you're activating the memories, and those memories are now in a vulnerable state; they're actually open to being modified before they're restabilized in long-term storage," explained Michael E. Saladin, PhD, professor, Department of Health Sciences and Research, College of Health Professions, Medical University of South Carolina, in Charleston.

"If you do a manipulation at that point... the theory is that you can impact those memories and change the behaviors associated with those memories," he was quoted as saying by Medscape Medical News [February 07, 2017].

According to Steve Ramirez, PhD, a neuroscientist at the Massachusetts Institute of Technology (MIT), at that critical moment of recall: "We can break into the time machine and really reverse-engineer it, we can really try to fix memories."

What this is telling us is that memory is not permanent. Recordings are built anew, every time we recall them. This process is called *reconsolidation*. It answers my description of fractal memory very beautifully! (page 11)

"We normally think of memory like a tape recorder or video of the past, but it's actually very reconstructive in nature," says Ramirez. "It's becoming more obvious that memory is really dynamic and it's very easily modifiable when [first] recalled."

Scientists are now studying how to tamper with memory using surgery, gene modification and drugs, such as propanolol (a beta-blocker). They are dealing with sick people, remember. We don't need such clumsy physical interventions, based on the mechanistic model. All it takes is a little skill and the knowledge contained in this manual! There is, as has been described, *a window for change that could be eased open at any time.* [*New Scientist*, vol 233, No 3111, 4 Feb 2017, p. 37]

This manual is a revolutionary way to ease open that window of change and effect some magic!

As the individual client gains in certainty and self-knowledge, we can eventually perform what we call *mass deconsolidation*. At this point, all memories have become plastic and fluid. The person only recalls things by re-creating the memory, if needed. You might think this is a very shaky way to recall things. That's the obvious thought.

But, hey! Another application of the 180-degree rule: when a person is able to function in this way, memory becomes much more reliable and, most importantly, under the person's control, instead of the other way round. It's selective and wise reconsolidation, where the memory is immediately put back in store in the stacks, fully fixed... without future liability.

No more restimulation (see page 89).

Cognosis

This is a neologism (invented word) for the process of coming to a new realization or understanding. These are the "Aha!" moments: "I just realized why I hate the color yellow!" or chagrin: "I've been wrecking a lot of people around me with these irrational outbursts, haven't I?"

The memories are modified to be more adaptive (intelligent) and functional. We are able to actually change a memory and have it reborn as something useful—or at least not disempowering. The ideal is to transform all memories in this meaningful way.

In fact we don't need to work on every single memoneme or destructive belief. Eventually the client becomes wise enough to "batch process" their stuff. Moments of cognosis add up; the person gets more and more insight into their own case. When this has continued long enough, you can expect a major shift, that is adopting a new viewpoint that sees things very differently. That's the start of transformation!

Flash Erase

It's worth understanding this phenomenon ahead of time. Sooner or later—depending on the individual case and his or her abilities—we reach a point where the client develops an ability just to look at some aspect of mind, event or thought sequence and "in a flash" dispose of it. Poof!

The maladjusted aspect of memory is instantly understood, re-configured for context, and sent back to storage. Thus it vanishes, exactly as the Rule Of Vanishment predicts.

Whole stacks of memories can be rendered less destructive this way. In time the person becomes... well, a new individual!

Punk Points: ···

- Almost all recovery and gain is from confronting and escaping the powers of the timeline and buried, charged memories.

- Boldness in giving instructions to the client is the key to success. The timeline will obey whatever instructions you give it, providing he client is engaged.

- Number of times through an unpleasant memory is a direct measure of how much charge is gotten off.

- This is not psychoanalysis or any other psychotherapy system where interpretations of experience are featured. We care not for opinions, only pulling off the charge. The client's thoughts will change as a result but we NEVER feed ideas to the client.

OK, time to dip a toe in the water!

CHAPTER 11

REVIVING HEDONIC MOMENTS

In Hypnoetics™ we achieve a great deal by running charge out of memonemes: those distressing and hurtful moments from the past that freeze our logic and stir up unwanted emotions. By clearing them and opening up the free mind space, we do miracles in re-framing a person's view of their life and history. We can change a person's whole viewpoint, sometimes at a stroke!

But for training our pilots—and for dishing out sheer delight—it's sometimes useful to revive ejoyable experiences. That's Punk! We retrieve and run what are technically known as *hedonic* experiences (pleasure times) in the same way we do with memonemes containing pain, negative emotions and altered behaviors. It's just that the outcome is different. We are restored and recover faith in the fact that life can be good!

For some people, that's a complete case transformation in itself!

Don't over do this, pleasurable though it can be. Sooner or later (usually sooner), the individual drops down into traumatic memories. Running pleasure has the unfortunate habit of triggering grief, misery and anger. "Why can't life always be this good?" can be a very disturbing question. It can throw up heavy charge.

Example: A case I ran some years ago was very startling. It was a woman in her 50s. She happily agreed to cooperate. She had no trouble finding a pleasure moment... a day at the beach when she was a child.

She could recall the smell of the salt air, the freshness of the breeze, sand between her toes and the sensation of riding on a donkey. I encouraged her to develop more and more perceptions. She actually licked her lips as I watched her, relishing the taste of an ice ream cone. Then she stopped.

"What happened next?" I prodded gently.

"Then we went home and my father tried to murder my mother..." she howled and burst into floods of tears. She sobbed and sobbed and sobbed. *It took me four hours of running to get all the charge off this terrifying incident.* It had lain virtually hidden for many decades but nevertheless contained all the violence of psychic trauma of the original event. It was as if the event were yesterday, not more than forty years ago.

Never accept that "time heals". It does not!

So, be warned. But don't let it put you off enjoyable experiences. They can be great feel-good explorations of mind and memory. Powerful memonemes run the mind, hidden in the background, not shallow memories of fun (more's the pity, sigh!)

Here's how it goes...

First Dip!

How to run a hedonic experience....

Grab your pal or mentor (or anyone handy and willing) and try this little drill with an enjoyable moment. Sit them comfortably and say:

Get relaxed and close your eyes (wait for compliance).

Recall a time that was pleasurable for you (wait till he or she does so).

Ask: *When was it?*

Ask: *Where were you?*

Then say:

Go back to [that date/time] *and bring the memory to life.* Be sure he or she has done so. If there is any doubt tell him or her to really be there, as if it is happening all over again. Revive means re-live it, make it NOW.

Tell me what you see or feel. Get brief details. Then:

Move to the beginning of this memory/episode/event and recall everything that happened.

Be sure he or she runs it all, to the end.

Then send them back through it again (good practice for later):

Return to the beginning of this memory; tell me when you are there.

Then instruct him or her to: *Scan through the event to the point where it ends and this time pay particular attention to the good feeling/positive emotions/sense of pleasure you felt.*

You will likely see your subject smile with pleasure. Only the most obtuse subject would not simply follow your instructions! But you must deliver your commands gently but firmly. Use a quiet business-like tone of voice; not so loud you are distracting.

Finally say:

Thank you. Please return to the present, open your eyes and look around.

If all went well, your subject is glowing with pleasure, congratulate yourself. You made the first steps to a very rewarding skill and possible career change.

You may find it helps to jot down the commands on a 3x5 index card. Later you will learn all commands by heart but for this exercise, just reading it works!

Practicing

We use this mainly as a means of practicing being able to competently manage and shift the timeline. It's great that you can enrich a case by doing it.

The emphasis then is on being sure that the client is "there", down the timeline, fully immersed in the moment, fully reliving it as NOW. The fact that it should evoke pleasure is just a bonus when using it to train pilots in this way.

Be sure to do the following:

Have him or her describe in the present tense. For example, "I am sitting looking across the room. I am feeling quite moved by the experience I have been reliving. On the wall I see a photograph and beside it is a lamp and I can hear the birds singing outside the window..."

Continue, including everyone who is present, what they say, their expressions, how you react and how they react.

Re-create the movements, smells, sound, tastes, the temperature, any music which was playing, and any feelings you have.

Go through it several times from the beginning to the end. When you have taken the scene as far as you want to go, let it fade away.

Concentrate on enjoyable or meaningful times from the past that you would like to pleasantly relive again. The negative ones will just fade away!

Altogether a very satisfying thing to do, to cash in the pleasure credits the individual has in the memory banks!

He Or She Can't Find Any Pleasure

Believe or not, I have encountered this phenomenon. What a life! No pleasures to remember in quiet moments of reflection. Such a person is, of course, very badly off on the Scale Of Emotional Health.

The solution is simple enough: have him or her invent it. Conceptually, he or she can get the idea that winning the lottery, say, would be pleasurable and mock up a picture and perceptions to go with it.

This will run just as well as a "real" event in life. All reality is an hallucination anyway, so what difference does it make?

There are endless wins and petty triumphs that could work: besting a guy at the office, kissing someone you love, moments of physical well-being, pride in accomplishment, and so on.

If even this turns out to be heavy going, use our very fine recall lists, coming up next.

Recall Prompts

Here is a list of delicious recalls we can use to get a person confronting their memories and not being scared of them. My thanks are to Peter Shepherd, of www.trans4mind.com, who took the trouble to compile them and graciously permitted me to use them.

Basically, you can choose any questions you like off the list. But obviously it is easier for you, as the pilot, if you just take them in turn!

Recall a time when you enjoyed yourself.

Recall a time when you earned some money.

Recall a time when you heard some good music.

Recall a time when you mastered something.

Recall a time when you got something you wanted.

Recall a time when you enjoyed a cozy fire.

Recall a time when you rode a bicycle.

Recall a time when you played with an animal.

Recall a time when you rearranged furniture.

Recall a time when you really knew what you were talking about.

Recall a time when you gave a successful demonstration or talk.

Recall a time when you straightened out a messy environment.

Recall a time when you felt good about the way you looked.

Recall a time when you enjoyed talking with someone.

Recall a time when you were acknowledged for a job well done.

Recall a time when you kept a promise.

Recall a time when you held somebody close.

Recall a time when you enjoyed exercising.

Recall a time when you drew a picture.

Recall a time when you helped somebody.

Recall a time when you won.

Recall a time when you met someone you got on well with.

Recall a time when you had a good time dancing.

Recall a time when you felt important.

Recall a time when you were having a good holiday.

Recall a time when you achieved something worthwhile.

Recall a time when you were enjoying a long walk.

Recall a time when you enjoyed working in the garden.

Recall a time when you had a good idea.

Recall a time when you kissed somebody you liked.

Recall a time when you laughed at a joke.

Recall a time when you painted something.

Recall a time when you felt enthusiastic.

Recall a time when you were with a friend.

Recall a time when you stood your ground.

Expanding the Sensate Awareness ·························

When the client can recall pleasurable experiences without much difficulty, repeat the above and look for earlier incidents of the same kind. That is, you ask:

1. Recall a time when...

2. Recall an earlier time when...

3. Recall the earliest time you can when...

You can extend these memory improvers even further by asking for different recall modalities, such as vision (seeing), audio (hearing), touch, smell, even moods!

For example: *Describe something you are seeing in the memory.*

Recall that sense in the experience and describe it, again in the present tense (For example, "I'm seeing lamp posts and parked cars...").

Senses List

1. Describe something you are seeing in that memory.

2. Describe something you are touching in that memory.

3. Describe a color that you see in that memory.

4. What is the temperature in that memory.

5. Describe the position of your body in that memory.

6. Describe a mood you are experiencing in that memory.

7. Describe something that you are hearing in that memory.

8. Describe something about the movement which is going on in that memory.

9. Describe something you are smelling in that memory.

Here are some more examples from the Recall List. You will never run out of ideas for pleasure recall:

Recall a time when you observed a birth.

Recall a time when you won something.

Recall a time when you completed a project.

Recall a time when you noticed you were growing up

Recall a time when you made an advancement in your career.

Recall a time when you got something published.

Recall a time when you reached a milestone.

Recall a time when you observed a child learning.

Recall a time when you observed something growing over time.

Recall a time when you felt a strong sense of identity.

Recall a time when you were anticipating a special event.

Recall a time when you were anticipating sexual pleasure.

Recall a time when you anticipated seeing someone after a long time apart.

Recall a time when you appreciated receiving an award.

Recall a time when you appreciated being accepted as leader.

Recall a time when you received unexpected respect.

Recall a time when you received encouragement from someone.

Recall a time when you received media attention.

Recall a time when you observed a wonderful view.

Recall a time when you admired some beautiful flowers.

Recall a time when you watched some wild animals.

Recall a time when you enjoyed looking at the sky.

A Good Recall Hack

If someone really has a poorly performing memory, you can try this excellent "recall something" hack:

It is a very simple but powerful repetitive process, which serves to break through the charge-barrier between the subject and his or her memory stacks. When this barrier is removed, it is much easier to be in the here-and-now, aware in the present moment.

Simply run: 'Recall Something' and demand the client serve up a memory, as quickly as he or she can! Then repeat the command, over and over.

Any memory will do, whether it is from one minute ago or from long ago. After a while you will run out of obvious stock memories and the recall "barrier" will become apparent. Keep going! Keep asking the question and keep the answers coming as quickly as possible (Important: do not dwell on any of the memories).

You could run this for yourself, if your memory leaves something to be desired. Simply record the phrase: 'Recall something' on a short endless-loop cassette or on your smartphone, as an MP3 loop. Play it back and get your memories moving! To start with, use say 5-second intervals, and gradually increase the rate to 1-second intervals.

Punk Points:

- We can clear charge from the timeline without even visiting unpleasant memories! We do it by recalling pleasure moments. By immersing the client in these, it's good practice for our core technique of bringing memories to life, which renders them plastic and changeable, as 21st century science shows.

- There is a slight risk of triggering unpleasant memories, while bathing in pleasurable ones. That's not your fault, as pilot. It's a function of the life your client has led till now! Don't beat yourself up. Just run what comes up. The librarian knows what she is doing!

- Some people are poor at general recall. These individuals can be helped by using pre-prepared lists of suggested recalls, used over and over. Each of the suggested recalls is pleasurable, so this is a nice experience for any one. Be sure to try Pete Shepherd's recall lists given here.

CHAPTER 12

THE HYPNOETICS™ TIMELINE TECHNIQUE

OK, you can do mild or harmless memories from the timeline. We now come to the target chapter of this book, relating how to do Hypnoetics™. This is the key Punk Psychology™ technique, around which the rest of the book revolves. It's your how-to guide.

The first two steps are simple enough:

1. Find someone to work on.

2. Find meaningful episodes, which will help the case recover their attention units.

The type of person you want to start with at first is someone in good mental shape. DO NOT start work with difficult cases, just because they are in a mess. Leave them till later or, better still, leave them alone altogether. This is not psychiatry or therapy. This is learning and mind expansion. It's really a kind of self-education for the individual.

But the first ten to twenty hours are for YOU, the learner. You need to make that clear to your volunteer client. If you are lucky and have a friend or colleague who wants to work with you and learn to pilot at the same time, that's great; you can work on each other, turn and turn about.

Get him or her to study this book and you are ready for action!

Otherwise, find someone who will grant you access to their mind and memory, for the purpose of learning the fundamental skills of Hypnoetics™. You should point out that there may be unpleasant emotions to encounter. But don't overplay this; assure your subject that you will be pushing beyond any negative emotions and they will soon vanish as part of the procedure.

Do not make promises you can't keep. Never say "I'll cure your migraine," or "I'll fix up your marriage, so she doesn't leave." You cannot know what lies behind these two conditions.

You can say, "Let's take a look at events from the past and see if they have any bearing on your migraines," because you can deliver on that undertaking and even to realize there's no connection between past history and the headaches still fulfills your promise!

Similarly, you could offer to "Work on your marriage and see if we can perhaps improve how you feel about the current state of affairs." That should be easy. Don't be naïve though. You might have a great breakthrough—about men or women in general—but then he goes home, the wife is in an hysterical angry mood and your subject is abused to the point of feeling worse. He loses all his gains.

It makes you look a failure.

Preliminaries

It can be a good idea to do a preliminary interview with your prospective client, especially if he or she is not known intimately to you. There may be stormy skies ahead! You need to know.

For that reason, I recommend you start with a series of simple questions, to gather data:

1. Have you had a serious or life-threatening illness? (run it)

2. Have you ever been hospitalized (in case they said NO in 1 above).

3. Have you ever felt in extreme danger? (run it)

4. Describe the moment in life you felt the most stressed (run it)

5. The Nadir: What do you consider the lowest point in your life? (get what started it and run it)

6. Did your life seem to go wrong at some particular point? From when? (get it worded and run it)

7. Has something happened that you don't ever want to happen again? (Get the episode and run it)

8. Is there an emotional pattern that seems to keep resurfacing? (get the earliest memory of it and run that)

From questions like these, you select likely tertiary or secondary memonemes. The nadir is a hot topic, usually. What exactly happened at that time? Or what got it started? (a person usually falls into the Nadir after some particularly harrowing experience).

You get a good wording for this, and ask the person if they are interested in running it. Rarely will he or she say "Naah!"

The Actual Procedure

OK, time to get going. You have chosen a key episode to run out. Proceed as follows:

1. Get a good wording for it (the client has to suggest the label for it or at the very least be fully comfortable with any suggestion of yours). Don't be too general; "quarrels with my boss" is vague. "Being made to look a fool at work" could run better. "The time I got fired from Westinghouse" would be an even better focus. Although it sounds a unique moment, there will be plenty of earlier related experiences on that thread, even down as far as being expelled in third grade!

2. Ask, *"When was it?"* Get a date, using any of the time tools on page 126.

3. Ask, *"Where was it?"* or *"Where were you at the time?"*

4. Say, *"Go back to* [date just given] *and revive the memory in full/bring it to life again."* For the first few attempts with a new client, you need to guide them gently: *"Travel back to that episode in your mind's eye. Make sure you are right back there, not just remembering it. Be there. Literally, bring it to life."*

4. When you are satisfied he or she is really there, ask: *"Tell me what happened."* You want brief narrative details. Then:

5. *"Move to the beginning of this memory/episode/event and talk me through it... bit by bit."*

Usually you will get a visual description but remember not everyone sees pictures. Some are audio people; they hear but don't see. Others are kinesthetics (touchy-feely), and so on.

Just take what the person says, no matter what sensory mode they are using.

If necessary, keep reminding them, with phrases like "Be there", "Being present", "Re-living it..." The exact instructions are not so important as the person being truly immersed. Listen for phrases like: "He's just coming round the corner..." rather than "He came round the corner" (wrong).

6. Be sure he or she runs it all, to the end.

Then send them through it again:

"Let's go through that again. Return to the beginning of the memory; tell me when you are there. Be fully immersed in what's happening."

7. Then instruct him or her *"Scan through the memory/event/episode to the point where it ends, this time paying special attention to...* (the emotions-what sounds you hear-what words were said-any colors-describe what she was wearing, etc. rotate the recall modalities each time through).

8. Keep the person cycling round. There are endless variants of the instructions. Just be clear that each time is a replay, a new run at it, in a new unit of time. So be careful he or she does not slip into remembering what they just did and start re-processing the short-term memory version. That will be them looking at themselves remembering and running the event from a few minutes earlier. No good. You want them back THEN.

Other than that, there's nothing to it!

Here's a quick tip: if the person has trouble getting the memory to mind clearly, ask: *"How long did it last?"* Having to "see" the whole thing, to identify the beginning to end points, often loosens the subconscious blackness and the details will appear, as if by magic!

9. If it gets stodgy, there is no lightening or relief, no emotional discharge and no

sense of recovery after a few times through, consider asking for an earlier related memory. If there is one, switch to running that. Only the client can decide what is related to what. If he or she thinks it's relevant, process it! Run it over and over.

This is when you sometimes drop into a past life memoneme. You ask "earlier related" to a pain in the chest; suddenly he or she is recalling being a Roman soldier, with an axe buried in the chest... Exciting times!

You can date these if you wish. But don't get intrusive or turn all academic. It doesn't matter. What is important is the freedom to express their memory, without censure or interference from you.

"The time I was a Roman soldier getting killed" is quite sufficient to date an episode, if you recall what you read earlier.

10. To end, say to him or her: *Thank you. Please return to the present, open your eyes and look around.*

Run some fresh reality (page 160), if you have learned that trick.

That's it, you're done. Rinse and repeat (often)!

Done well, this is a killer procedure. I call it my "Make It NOW" technique (MINT). The intensity of really "being there NOW" is what makes it work so well.

Handles •••

Sometimes you get what we call a "handle" on a memoneme. The person does something that makes it clear there is a memory surfacing. Thus, he or she might start breathing strangely. What do you do? You ask the client to breathe that way deliberately; it will accelerate the appearance of the MIMP and its content.

He or she might say something out loud. "God, what are you doing here?" Ask them to repeat this phrase, out loud, over and over. The context will quickly make itself known; a visual will appear, with someone saying, "God, what are you doing here?" (that's a trick from Alfred Korzybski and his General Semantics).

You may hear a long sigh. Here's a quick tip: when you hear a client sigh deeply, know that grief is nearby. He or she will be blubbering in just a few minutes!

Watch for the person changing personality... or even changing shape! Yes, it does happen. As the violent force of a memoneme moves in on him or her, it can truly distort the body. Of course the normal shape will resume, as soon as you have flattened the memoneme.

Finally, here's a weird one. But those of you who are tuned in to metaphysical phenomena will quickly grasp it: you (the pilot) start to see MIMPs before your client does. He's thinking about it and you've already got the picture!

This can extend to picking up on unpleasant pains and sensation too. Nothing is ever bad enough to make you want to back off. But quite often *you* will feel a pain in a certain part of your body, several minutes before he or she remarks on that *same feeling* they are experiencing.

It's rather remarkable.

Now, just a few warnings...

Forbidden

The following are complete No-Nos. You are abusing the Hypnoetics™ code if you try to work on these people:

1. Known criminals who have not declared a reform. People who continue to do bad things seldom make any worthwhile gains. Do NOT try to rehab such a person with your knowledge and skills.

There is one other aspect you might not think of: he or she could tell you something that puts you in danger. I had a client once who admitted hiring a killer to knock off his wife. The deed was never done but the money was paid over. I was suddenly an accessory to a conspiracy to murder. Fortunately, being a qualified MD, I was able to stand on my secrecy principles. But if you know something about a major crime or murder, even a doctor is not supposed to remain silent.

Bear that in mind.

2. A psychiatric case who tends to be unstable. I repeat from earlier that these are not the people you want to learn on. The broader subject of Supernoetics® has far more advanced techniques that can, applied correctly, destimulate psychiatric patients to the point where they can live reasonably normal lives. But just plunging them into a formative memoneme is the last thing you want to do. The whole reason he or she is manic, psychotic, schizoid, or whatever, is that he or she is already stuck in powerful memonemes from the past.

There's another important factor: *almost ALL psychiatric patients are physically ill, not mentally ill.* My landmark book *Holistic Psychiatry* gives extensive information on solving mental distress with physical healing. Correctable factors, like food allergies, toxin overload, hormonal imbalances and stealth pathogens account for almost all symptoms that psychiatrists see. They just don't bother investigating nutrition, hormone status and other factors, because they don't believe in it. Psychiatrists tend to be lazy. All they care about is prescribing psycho-active drugs, which poison and overwhelm the mind's function.

Remember the metaphor of the brain as a smart phone (page 5)? Modern psychiatric treatments are the equivalent of hitting the phone with a hammer and then saying, "See, no more unpleasant messages." It's kind of sick, actually.

So stay clear.

3. Persons taking heavy mind-altering drugs. This includes people on psychiatric medication but also individuals who regularly take mind-altering drugs (yes, that includes marijuana, which is NOT considered harmless in Supernoetics® and Hypnoetics™).

If you get to work with such a case who wants help (actually asks for it), you must insist they end all drug taking and leave a wash-out period of at least three weeks. If they are taking antipsychotic medication, such as SSRIs, this is a tricky issue. The patient must inform their doctor they want to stop and ask for help. Most often, the doctor will believe in the effect of anti-depressants, even though none have ever been proven really effective (and SSRIs have been proven over and over NOT to work, but they still get prescribed because of massive dishonest spinning by the pharmaceutical companies who manufacture them).

Bottom line: you must never advize a person to stop taking medications. You could be in big legal trouble.

4. Persons who are currently in turmoil. If someone is undergoing a messy divorce, declaring bankrupt, just been diagnosed with a malignant tumor, been fired and struggling to find re-employment, etc. you will find him or her hard to help. That does not mean they are difficult cases per se, but that life is kicking them so hard, you can't cheer them up fast enough. The next day could put an end to hours of determined work by you.

It's can be very disheartening.

Better to wait until the real-world events settle down and then patch up him or her! It will be less frustrating for all concerned.

Meantime, you could coach him or her, using Supernoetics® methods for creating or restoring the ideal life. Remember, *knowledge about what to do is almost as valuable as mind power and feeling good*. No matter how troubled he or she is by circumstances, if a person knows what to do for the best and keeps doing it, no matter how they feel inside, it will all come out right in the end. That's why we call it "healing knowledge" in Supernoetics®.

5. Strong religious fanatics. I have no stomach for these people personally. I tend to give them a wide berth. Everything you say or do gets twisted into some words or other supposedly in the Bible. It's like talking to a robot, not a human being. You talk, they spout scriptures. This is not good for the path of spiritual growth and awareness.

These people have been literally brain-washed, and believe that the more fanatical and obedient they are, the more surely they will be "saved". This applies to many religions of course, including Islam, Judaism, Hinduism and even Buddhism. That's not to say the religions in themselves are bad but the droning semi-psychotic state some people get into, when controlled by the priest classes, is pretty crazy. You may have seen sad pictures of young boys, rocking backwards and forwards over their Torah, or men standing with arm held high for months (until the fibers of the arm make it permanent) as a "gesture to God". And don't get me started on terrorists or suicide bombers, who have been controlled to murderous proportions by some sick, impotent mullah.

Keep well away from political and religious activism. The test? They want to convert you! That's the beginning of intolerance.

Punk Points: ···

- We look for moments in a person's past that were very stressful. By sending him or her back to that time—travelling "in the mind's eye"— and re-processing that experience in a vivid "now" manner, we can bleed off charge from the memoneme. Enough persistence (enough passes through it) will bring relief.

- If not, then there are earlier related memories. We track these down and clean them up. Sometimes we are lucky and get right to the "root" of the thread, deal with that, and the whole trait or thought process reverts to normal. Likely as not, the individual will never think of these things again, without being reminded.

- "Handles" is a colloquial term for the many manifestations that indicate charged material is coming to the surface, such as sighs, odd movements, and verbal content (charged phrases that are part of the memoneme). We can sometimes have the person repeat the action or phrase deliberately, to speed up the reconsolidation process, for faster running and faster relief.

- Don't try to work on very difficult cases. Hypnoetics™ and the other simple tools of Punk Psychology™ are designed to be of help to the average person, not to salvage those who have backed themselves into extreme difficulties. Criminals and psychotics are best handled by changing society to something more caring and responsible, rather than trying to deal one at a time with wrecked individuals.

CHAPTER 13

FURTHER ADVICES

Apart from the five interdicts at the end of the previous chapter, there are very few DOs and DON'Ts in Hypnoetics™. Here are a few guidelines, that are important. They will steer you clear of the rocks and make your client's passage smoother.

First and foremost, avoid being judgmental. You must not say anything that implies criticism, invalidation or contradiction to what the client says. Nothing closes down communication faster than judgment or criticism! Just don't do it.

It is important that your voice remains at all times non-emotional and non-engaged—neutral—or zero. Maintain a polite business-like tone of voice, tempered with the normal rules of kindness and compassion.

You must be able to tolerate ANY reaction, emotion, words or attack from a client, without flinching, snarling back or reacting in any way. Things occasionally get hairy and your calm is the anchor that keeps things on an even keel.

Yelling and screaming? Just say, "Return to the beginning of this episode and tell me when you are there?" as unemotionally as you would say, "Please pass the salt," at the dinner table!

You must never tell the person what to think, what you have observed on the case or make comments that imply judgment. It can severely disturb a case. Moreover you must never explain a client's case in any way, ever, no matter even if he or she demands it.

Don't break or change appointments, once made, except in a real emergency. To have appointments cancelled or re-arranged makes a person feel unimportant or like furniture that can be shuffled around.

Keep yourself looking presentable. Never show up for a breakout looking dirty, disheveled, unkempt, lacking sleep or with a hangover that shows you are casual or disrespectful. The client/psychonaut surrenders a lot to you; make sure you are worthy of that trust. Even as a beginner, you must act professionally.

Carry yourself with presence and bearing at all times, remembering you are you are among a tiny minority of beings who understand the workings of the mind and how to repair and re-engineer it.

Get work done on yourself, in return for what you do for others. It's important to keep your own case in good shape. Remember, the better your own case, the better pilot you will be; the more insight you will have. Also you are less likely to be stirred up by what's on display in the seat opposite!

Do not discuss any of your cases outside of the breakouts, except with your trainer. Interesting, alarming or bizarre stories are not fodder for discussion and amusement in the tavern or at table. Not even anonymously, because stories may be passed around and the client may recognize him or herself and feel betrayed, even though—to others—it's "anonymous".

Similarly, case examples shared with you in training are NOT for public discussion. These revelations too can get back to the case.

Avoid "small talk" with your client, beyond the necessary minimum, such as meal breaks, transport to and from the office etc. Small talk always carries the potential of accidentally tripping a reaction or upsetting the client, without any potential for healing a case. Don't play with fire!

This injunction is one of the reasons we don't like spouses piloting each other: it's almost impossible for a couple not to stir up each other's charge between sessions. That's makes piloting your spouse later somewhat tricky. It may be you that he or she is annoyed with and you have waste time healing the crash of accord! (our term for an upset or quarrel).

Heavy Going ···

If the person has run into some heavy trauma memories, make sure he or she is in good shape before you let them go home. Make sure that he or she is warned to be careful of traffic and machinery. Forbid driving a vehicle unless *absolutely necessary* and then only if he or she agrees to proceed slowly and avoid all confrontational driving.

Later in this section, you can see a few rescue and repair techniques, such as drifting back to the Now, via some tasty pleasure moments, or shifting the person's viewpoint on high, to look down on themselves being themselves.

Even if things have gone well, this sort of injunction could be important for safety. Very great amounts of psychic mass, energy and debris can be shifted by our piloting, considerably altering the immaterial being's perspective and therefore impairing judgment of distances. Expect some temporary clumsiness.

The body has the same dimensions as before but the being has often expanded and is "out there" and the client may not realize that all previous estimations of distance and effort are invalid, unless this is explained.

Be patient: In a world dedicated to haste, where even instant gratification is too slow for some, you need to go gently. You may not get a miracle running the first memoneme. That's fine. Sometimes it takes 10 – 20 hours before the client starts winning. Just keep pulling off charge and sooner or later, you will get a stunning change in the person.

It's like doing the mind's laundry! Scrub everything clean. Hypnoetics™ is the punk soap that removes even the most stubborn stains in the mind!

Here's to a spotless memory!

Keep Up To Date ···

Keep up to date with the latest research and techniques, appropriate to your grade of piloting. Continue to practice and expand your skills, with retraining as appropriate. If you stop piloting, recognize that indirect charge has got to your case and get yourself fixed up so you are once again willing to help others. You have exceptional and valuable skills that should not be wasted.

Do nothing to exaggerate or boast or make wild claims for Supernoetics®, Hypnoetics™, the Punk Psychology™ Project or piloting. Do not engage in any kind of conversation or gossip that is derogatory to Supernoetics®, myself or my family or assigns. Protect your heritage!

Finally, if you encounter any unusual case reaction or occurrence be sure to report it up the line. Remember you are part of a knowledge-building tribe.

Can We Do This On Ourselves?

The quick answer is NO! Sure, you can run pleasure moments alone, and get charge off that way. We can do love, gratitude and forgiveness on ourselves. More of that later.

But when it comes to heavy disturbing memonemes—trying to run those on ourselves—it just doesn't work. Think it through for a moment: we dwell on unpleasant memories all the time, turning them over in our mind. It doesn't do any good, does it? They remain unpleasant thoughts. Churning them around inside your head doesn't heal them!

You could end up really stuck in the past, in other words you've effectively hypnotized yourself. You become a somnambulist and would not be safe around a hot stove or machinery!

So don't bother trying it. Instead find a buddy and take turn and turn about, working on each other's case.

The difference comes when you have mastered the use of a GSR meter. That's a game changer. With the meter to support you, guide you and, in effect, dialogue with you, it's like having an extra intelligence center in the conversation. That can work!

You can learn how to do self-piloting, as it's called, in later studies. For now, just do what it says in this book and get very good at it!

When the Going Is Really Tough ·····························

Sometimes, a case can be very ruffled and you may want to end off because of that. Try not to. We prefer to work with Robert Frost's admirable maxim: *the best way out is the way though.* Just keep going and it will usually turn off any ugly flare up of feelings or emotions.

Once in a while you will get a client into a very heavy dramatization. Primary memonemes are pretty wild stuff, when you trigger one; the furniture flies, the air turns blue and sometimes clothes get ruffled or torn.

This is very rare. You may never see it. If you do, remember the simple Hypnoetics™ rule: *keep going while it keeps coming!* This is a version of the old homeopathic principle: "Whatever provokes will also heal". What turns the drama on is the key to what turns it off. Repetition will weaken its grip and eventually all the energy drains out of the memoneme.

Once the dramatization has ceased, you may then end off and seek advice from a more knowledgeable trainer.

Much more common is to have your case dissolved into floods of tears, sobbing and other hysterics. On the GSR meter, he or she may fling down the electrodes and attempt to leave the room (you must never let that happen).

Agree to stop the action and remedy any unwanted feelings; do not agree anything was wrong or the need to end off. It's the person's case that is hitting them, remember, not a mistake on your part.

We also have structured repair lists, which need a meter. We call off likely triggers and by choosing the definitive meter read, point out the source of the indirect charge. The whole drama will switch off in seconds. It's a version of Deep-IS (page 16), where the truth blows away the hurt.

I've seen a case, whose face was as black as thunder, stop scowling and laugh in less than a minute, after finding the indirect charge that was stirred up!

You need to be a Supernoetics® Level 2 pilot to do that, however. If you are just starting out, as in the Punk Psychology™ Project, here are some simple tips as to how to calm everything down before you send your client home or allow him or her to drive a vehicle.

Repairs ···

1. Pleasure Moments (see page 136).

Drag him or her out of the violent memoneme towards present time, using a pleasure moment. Explain what you are going to do and then just say:

- *Locate a pleasurable moment nearer to present time.*

- *When was it? Move to* [whenever is was]. *Really be there.*

- *Talk me through it. Tell me what you see and feel...* and so on, making sure he or she becomes properly immersed in it and starts to lighten up or smile.

Then you could find another one. Finish up with a little of the following...

2. Run what we call "Fresh Reality".

That means more connectivity with the current physical surroundings. Some workers use the term "grounding", which sums it up nicely. Our good friend Rolf Dane has come up with several simple commands which may prove useful:

- "Look at that (room object)," vase, table, picture, wall, etc., etc.

- "Point out something."

- "Where is the (room object)?" (clients points.)

- "Look around here and find something you would like to remain in place."

- "Point out something in this room you could confront."

- "What else is that (indicated object)?"

- "What is the condition of that (room object)?"

- "Find an object you are not in (inside)."

Symptoms like grogginess, sleepiness and the like, point towards a need for running Fresh Reality. It is also routinely used at the end of a work session (breakout) to get the client extroverted and back in the Now again. The pilot takes just one of the above lines and runs it maybe 10-20 times, until the client feels more alert and present.

3. Another neat item in your "toolbox" is 6-Directions.

It's a set of cycling commands (one after the other, then back to the beginning again, through them again, over and over, till you get relief). Get a description of the unpleasant feeling, mass or pain that seems most prominent, and then instruct the client as follows:

1. Put (item) above you.

2. Put (item) below you.

3. Put (item) out to the right.

4. Put (item) out to the left.

5. Put (item) out in front of you.

6. Put (item) behind you.

The distance the item is put from the client can be changed from time to time. "Put the item two meters (six feet) above you", etc. for several rounds.

6-Directions makes the person exert control over these items that have influenced his/her life and way of thinking negatively. Once the person can take control over such mental energies and masses, by moving them around at will, they cease to have much effect on the person's case.

Another way to use 6-Directions, if things have become all confusing, is to simply take an item from the memoneme content, the car you were driving in, say, or the weapon the soldier held in his hand, or whatever, and run 6-D on that. Take some item you are *sure* is in the incident and flatten it with 6-D. You can do several items like that, each to a flat point, and sooner or later the whole event sorts itself out and you can return to the original action.

Or at least end off without the person left stuck in the memoneme.

4. Pendulation (also known as Before and After)

If a memory is really too horrific to face—the person simply can't and won't look at it—then this simple technique will gradually raise his or her confront. It's a version of what clinical psychologist Peter Levine, author of *Waking The Tiger* (1997), calls pendulation. It's like a pendulum, swinging backwards and forwards

For over 30 years I've just called it Before-and-After.

We simply ask the person to remember happenings just before and just after the unconfrontable trauma. In extreme cases, he or she may not want to remember anything for weeks or months before or after some dreadful event.

Leave it open at first:
1. *Recall something before the episode/shock moment.*
2. *Recall something after the episode/shock moment.*

But gradually we bring them closer and closer: "Remember something a week before/after...", "Now remember something an hour before/after... "Now remember something just moments before/after it started", "What's the first thing you can comfortably remember after the event?" and so on.

Gradually, as we get closer and closer, you will see clear physiological reactions. If you are using the eMind Sensor™ you will see more and more intense reaction. Then, almost inevitably, he or she will drop into the really traumatic memory and start to process it.

5. Feel it Back

This is a great tool. If someone is really into something heavy (shaking with remembered fear, sobbing, etc.) use this. If something too strong to work with is encountered, stop running it and switch to Feel It Back. If the person is resisting the emotion or feeling, use Feel It Back. Again, like Tool 3, it's giving somebody the chance to gain control over their emotions.
1. *"Put that emotion/feeling into the wall."*
2. *"Now, feel it back."* Used repeatedly, over and over.

Don't say, "Take it back"; the client just feels it emanating from the wall and handles it from a distance!

The pilot can pick other big and solid objects than walls, of course. Don't go on too long after a few rounds; check if the feeling is now manageable.

6. The Glass Elevator

If all else fails, you can use this technique. It comes from the Supernoetics® model *The Complex Of Self* (chapter 17). We are an animal or "creature" self at the base (ground floor); above that are increasingly airy and non-material layers of self (upper floors). We can get the upset client to rise above what has been happening and look down on themselves, like in a glass elevator! We use the command, "Go up on high and look down on the scene you are in; see yourself being yourself."

This pulls them right out of the suffering human being they see below. It's quite incredible. The human self is sobbing and wailing, with gnashing of teeth, yet the self as a higher being looks down on that, completely uninvolved in the emotion.

It's a place of being detached or "dissociated", as opposed to being immersed or "associated", as they call it in NLP.

The self above is sometimes even amused, thinking, "He'll get over it soon. Serves him right. But he'll be wiser for it!" Yes, *that* detached!

When the emotion has calmed, you have a choice: end off, or gently lower the person back into the associated position, when he or she will feel the emotions again. But this time less intense and more manageable. You can always send them back "upstairs" again, if you need to.

Note: Buddha used the term mindfulness for watching the self from outside; Georges Gurdjieff called it "self-remembering".

Ending Off

Well, here are plenty of tools to prevent you getting stuck. One of them should dig your client out of the overwhelming charge and get him or her back to the here-and-now. If not, proceed to try another one.

Remember, I told you, that Hypnoetics™ is really all about managing and manipulating the timeline.

You'll soon develop a real skill and feeling for where a person is on their timeline. Most people start out not completely in the Now, of course. So don't expect any better than where he or she started from.

The acid test is whether he or she wants to do more. Mostly, clients enjoy a thrilling ride and think it's part of the fun, which of course it is. Cases are incredibly resilient, on the whole. But some people are a little bit nervous and frail. Don't push him or her so hard next time.

Finally, here's a really simple and under-used remedy: *If all else fails, sleep is the number one restorative.* Send your client home to bed, with an undertaking to return in the morning. Things will dissipate after a good night's sleep.

Punk Points: ··

- To get the best results for the people you are helping, you need to develop a degree of professionalism. At least you must manifest calm and control, even if the situation becomes a little challenging!

- Don't engage in small talk or distractions. NEVER be judgmental and never explain anything to your subject/client. He or she has to work it out for themselves. "Explaining" things never leads to real insights or cognosis and often makes matters worse.

- Trying to do it by yourself, on yourself, is not recommended. It takes two. We dwell on unpleasant memories all the time, turning them over in our mind and it doesn't do any good, does it? They remain unpleasant thoughts. Learn from this fact. Find some buddies and take turn and turn about, working on each other.

- If the going get tough, remember the simple Hypnoetics™ rule: *keep going while it keeps coming!* This is a version of the old homeopathic principle: "Whatever provokes will also heal".

- Finally, there are some killer tricks in the "toolbox" that will help pull a person out of any discomfort. Just stay calm and put these tools to work!

CHAPTER 14

SENSATE AWARENESS

The medical term "psychosomatic" refers to feelings which are pressed upon the body by some force within the mind. Note I do not say that these feelings are delusions or unreal, only that the mind places them in the body.

The psychosomatic label is avoided here, since it has become somewhat pejorative. The general use of the word is to imply a merely fantasy feeling, which doesn't exist at all in reality. Individuals who experience psychosomatic disease are supposed to be not really ill.

This is a very silly and ignorant distinction, of which almost all doctors are guilty. It supposes that "real" pain is different in nature from that which is illusory. A moment's thought will indicate that all pains are felt "in the mind", whether or not they go via nerve pathways in the first instance.

Today's enlightened view (unfortunately not shared by the majority of the medical profession) is that all the important functions of the mind and body, all that we do and feel, and nearly all that happens to us, including sensations within the body, are the result of the working of programs or meta-programs in the mind. This includes pain, disease, unwanted emotion, unacceptable habits, destructive behaviors, false beliefs, various urges and desires and every thing that makes us feel guilty.

Even dreaded cancer can be regarded as a psychically-induced malady and most of the remarkable recoveries can be attributed to resolving psychological conflicts. The addressing of such issues is rightly considered to be a crucial part of any intelligent medical treatment.

The fact is, our body talks to us. If we take the trouble to listen, our bodies tell us something is wrong, a troubling thought is pressing, a physical condition is being ignored, some flow or communication is blocked.

We call this internal signaling phenomenon *sensate awareness*: being aware of sensations within.

You ignore the signals at your peril: they are never without a significant cause and are remarkably accurate. To ignore the messages as "unimportant" is as foolish as ignoring a red stop signal while driving in traffic.

It's Universal

Everyone is familiar with sensate awareness; it's just the label that may be unfamiliar. We all share expressions like an "adrenalin rush", "butterflies in the stomach", a "heavy heart", a "blood rush" (rage), a "gut feeling" or a "lump in the throat". These are the body's feedback to what we are thinking and doing.

Here are several more for you: "I caught my breath", "My heart sank", "My blood turned to ice", "It gave me goose bumps just to think about it", "I had a heavy feeling in the pit of my stomach."

Surprisingly, so also are: "I went blank", "My thoughts were all confused", "I panicked", "His touch caused me to melt".

You will quickly see that any and all of these sensations can be caused by a thought, just as surely as by an injury, a microbe or a parasite!

Emotions too are merely a kind of sensate feedback. We experience them according to what we are doing and what our circumstances tell us. Emotions seem to be a sort of shorthand coding for how we think we should react and behave.

The more unpleasant and inappropriate emotions we can label negative emotions. The obvious ones are anger, fear or grief or these can be refined into more subtle gradations, such as uncertainty, confusion, hostility, pique, apprehension, beautiful sadness, tenseness or despair.

Above all, don't forget that sexual arousal is a kind of sensate feedback. This may seem obvious during the sexual act. But also there are many variants of sexual feeling we enter when talking about sex, being titillated in some way or anticipating later arousal and orgasm. This response can take place in public, fully clothed and without another member of the opposite sex present. It is definitely sexual experience "in the mind".

If you want to learn more about this aspect of self-analysis, read *Focusing* by Eugene T. Gendlin, Bantam Books, New York, (revised edition) 1981.

Using Sensate Awareness As A Tool

Just as focusing on the feedback signals of the measuring instruments in "biofeedback training" enables one to change physiological functions like pulse rate, blood pressure and electrical conductivity of the skin, so can focusing on the sensate feedback make us aware of the mental programs which underlie our feelings and reactions and so enable us to drag them into conscious view.

Feeling what our body is signaling to us gives us access to a vast deal of information about the mind.

More important to us in Hypnoetics™, is that sensate awareness is a way to get much more engagement when case running. Instead of just recounting the experience as a memory (15% release) or running it by "being there and reliving it" (60% release), we can increase the discharge rate and therefore the level of relief to 90 – 95% by having the client process and re-live many other aspects of the mental imprint (MIMP). Indeed that why we use the term MIMP. Much more is imprinted at the time of the memory recording that mere thoughts and impressions for recollection latter.

There is often a LOT of force in a MIMP. It can be enough to distort the person's body or face (leaning to one side; face unbalanced to one side or flattened). There may be many feelings, such as warmth or cold, trembling, heaviness, can't move or excitement.

How Do We Use This?

Two main ways:

When opening a case for the first time, we might ask especially for any pains, feelings, emotions, aversions, obsessions, attitudes, or any persistent physical symptoms or even unwanted mental energy (such as fatigue) that the client is aware of. Often, if you question the point, these will be found to directly associate with certain physical feelings within the body. We can ask: "What part of your body do feel that hostility? [emotion, sensation, attitude...etc.]"

Getting a good list of such subjective symptoms can be a great way to approach a startup case. It's made even more powerful if you add in beliefs and decisions. Life is often turbulent and at such times a person is liable to make a choice or decision, or formulate a belief, that later comes to haunt him or her and cannot easily be identified and got rid of.

The second way to use sensate awareness is to clear more charge from incidents that we are running. A person may just stick to memory recall and "thoughts" about what was happening. Often you will see him or her experiencing an unpleasant symptom. But it may not be mentioned. Don't be afraid to clarify what you are seeing or hearing and what the client is experiencing.

Ask leading (but not pejorative or dismissive) questions like, "Is there any specific feeling associated with running this memory?" We clarify what and where and then ask the client to run the episode again and again, each time trying to create the feeling or sensation. "Get it again... Get it again..." and so on, until the feeling is exhausted and drained out of the MIMP.

"Where in your body do you feel that heaviness?" and so on. "Get that feeling in your [body part]."

Often while running an episode, the client will mention something new, without you asking: "That time I felt really sad..." Well, have him or her run it again, "Feel the sadness, feeling really weighed down with sadness, make it come, don't fight that sadness."

"Don't fight it," is actually another workhorse phrase that you should learn and use.

Be alert and watch for signs too, like a sudden groan or jerk, that may denote an unpleasant bodily awareness. Question these (what just happened then?) and add them to your breakout worksheet. You will often end up running with a sensate awareness that was not even present when you started on the memory or encounter.

Decisions and Beliefs Too

The pilot could gain a lot of extra traction on a case by asking if there was a significant decision made as a result, or if a belief arose, due to a heavily charged episode. We can use the repeater technique, in just the same way: "Get that thought again..." or "Get that decision again..." and again and again type approach, until there is no more change.

Having him or her say a phrase out loud is often a great way to get traction or increase the client's immersion on the MIMP you are working on.

This is a cognitive step, meaning it's more about thoughts and reasoning. But here's the important point to remember: the decision or belief holds its power from the charge present in the initial incident.

But in the end, thoughts and postulates, decisions and beliefs are like real things and will *persist* until cleared in piloting.

So whatever happens, once you start releasing the charge, any decision will be weakened, any belief seem less tenable, any behavior will seem more and more foolish or pointless, as a result of clearing off charge.

Less Obvious Sensations

There are other important but less obvious aspects of processing sensate awareness. The MIMP of the incident may contain the pressure to push away or hold onto something or someone. There may be a traction effort (an effort to pull towards); or to pull away (withdraw from); or to hold something still and prevent movement.

Probably the most important aspect of sensate awareness processing is the matter of forceful contact with the physical world. I'm talking about actual impact, for example in an episode of injury or trauma. It may be a distorting (deforming) injury and you will sometimes see this manifest on the person's body. The client's description of the episode will alert you to the possibility of physical violence. You want that feeling identified, isolated and processed carefully, until it vanishes. The sensation of being hit hard can be relived and processed, as with any other feeling. Don't stop till it is thoroughly exhausted from the MIMP.

You will only find out about these sensations by asking directly about them and getting your client to feel the feeling. The extra charge taken off, shown as more differential if you are using biofeedback, and more obvious case gain, make it well worth our while processing physical feelings of this order, as well as purely narrative impressions.

The thing is, after a few runs through, we start asking the client about these sensate awareness extras. They are a goldmine. You can release bucketloads more charge than with other simple psychotherapy systems!

Positive Feelings

Let us not forget that positive sensate feedback exists too. In its way it can by just as valuable as the uncomfortable kind. Feelings of excitement, thrill, warmth and heart's-ease can all signal that something is good, rewarding and healthful.

Important life-principle: In the same way that we can become aware of negative feedback and use it to correct disharmony, so we can use the corresponding positive effects to reinforce whatever is beneficial to us.

Positive signals are really pointing to the truth, just as negative feelings point to lies and disharmony.

Punk Points:

- The mind sends constant signals to us, via our body. We can choose to ignore these "messages" but that's not very bright. Even cancer might be a "message" that you are not living a harmonious lifestyle.

- In piloting these body signals are called *sensate awareness* and are regarded as a very valuable aid to finding and cleaning out charged memories (memonemes).

- Emotions too are a kind of sensate awareness. All emotions have an important bodily component (the *feeling*).

- We can ask our client to deliberately provoke and repeat the sensate awareness, over and over, to swell the experience of the memory, "Feel it again... and again" etc.

- Even pleasurable sensations are a kind of sensate awareness, telling us something is going right!

- Force, violence, impact and injury in a memory (memoneme) are what keeps it in place. The force can hold down the thoughts or feelings... and *vice versa*.

CHAPTER 15
SIGNS OF PROGRESS

Knowing When To Quit

One of the very important skills we teach pilots is simply *knowing when to quit*. Or at least, when to take a break! Sometimes the results are outstanding, the client consumed with delight, or overwhelmed with excitement, and it would be inappropriate to continue. It can even happen that the person is so blown out, they temporarily can't access their case, so nothing useful can be done anyway, until he or she settles down.

Better to take a break, let him or her enjoy their win, and come back to these things later. Nothing is lost by this and the interlude does not allow them to relapse. What really happens is that he or she processes the initial success and then pulls in more related charge, which now also needs addressing. This process repeats over and over, until he or she has no more available charge to pull in. The issue or topic has gone flat. It's no longer a problem. Usually this is reflected in the fact that the client has found new abilities and the old issue no longer arises.

Very satisfying.

Here is a review of what we call quit-points (QPs), that is: moments when we choose to end off, for one reason or another. The only thing we try to avoid at all costs is quitting because the person is finding the going tough.

If you have moved on to GSR metered flights, that will also help you decide when to stop. After tons of differential, the person looks happy and the needle has gone null or IDLE. That's the time to end off for now.

In escalating order of "Wow!" these are some quit points you should look out for.

1. The client is running out of energy. Simple but obvious. It can be very exhausting at times, dealing with mental energies. Moving and processing them sometimes feels like moving rocks around! It's tiring. You can continue later, after a break that can be short, like for a coffee, a bite to eat, or a nap—or longer, like a good night's sleep, or until he or she feels rested enough to continue.

2. Also not technically a quit point: The time that was planned for the flight is over and you are not in the middle of something charged. It is OK to end the flight early at this point, in order to keep the schedules of both client and pilot in good working order, and continue it at the next appointment.

Below is a list of genuine possible quit points:

3. A whole topic, issue, or episode (event) is discharged and the client feels released and good about it. This is the commonest reason to end a flight. All is good; case progressing well. Time to move on to the next episode or topic. Or "See you next time!"

4. The previous quit point may be a resolution only from the client's point of view. But if you are doing multiple-viewpoint Hypnoetics™ (chapter 166), there is still the need to run the viewpoint of others involved. Flattening or fully discharging another's viewpoint, with a good result, is also a handy moment to quit. Again it may mark the end of an issue or topic or be a good moment to end off the flight.

You will spot these basic QP moments easily, as times when there is a new insight or realization (see *cognosis* below), an upsurge in mood, healthy smiles or laughter, a gain in certainty or ability.

4. If the result of what you are doing results in a really huge, earth-shattering or life-changing realization, then the whole flight needs to end. The client is floating on cloud nine and grinning from ear to ear. Trying to continue may invalidate the big win.

5. Similar to item 1, we have what may be called a "hard work QP": The client has completed a big chunk of work that really cost him energy, and we end the flight, rather than take on something new in the time

remaining, to avoid a situation where we would have to leave off in the middle of something charged because the client has run out of steam.

6. We end any flight, even if we are sure there is still charge, if the client is so "blown out" that he cannot contact it. We need to make a break until he has come down to Earth and can do more piloting. This can take minutes, hours, days; sometimes even weeks or months.

We have to end the flight, even if it was short, because in this condition he or she will not be able to contact his or her remaining case. But don't make the mistake of assuming that is the completion of our protocol at this point. That's a mistake often made by other workers and other teachings. To not come back to the topic and check if it is still loaded may be to leave a lot of charge unhandled because it has not been addressed and can be triggered again when the client has come down from his cloud!

7. Out of body (exterior) QP: Sometimes the client reports that he went out of his body, or we recognize it by some statement he makes, like suddenly being bigger than before, or the room having become much brighter. If this is new to the client and very exciting to him, it is also a reason to end the flight. Basically it is another version of the "blown out QP" - a positively overwhelming experience.

8. Whole subject flattened: The charged subject, traumatic incident, identity clash or other item we were working on is no longer charged for the client and he is either in a pleasant calm mood, or in a great mood and excited about a positive change that he experienced. This can happen before we have done all the steps of the protocol we have started, and the rule is that we are ending here and skip the remaining steps.

It would be a mistake to assume a subject is done, when we are really looking at a "blown out" client. It will not be a disaster if we move on to the next subject, but there is a big risk that it now appears uncharged when it is really not, simply because the client cannot, at that moment, feel any of his charge! So it is better to have one too many flight with an early end than one too few.

You will readily see that some of these quit points are difficult to call. The main thing is you will not screw anyone up by making the wrong choice, so don't angst about it! You will develop more skill and knowing with practice.

Hopefully you will be able to get yourself into a mentoring situation, where someone more experienced can guide you.

Now let's move on to the grander topic of case gain.

Case Gain Definition

Change for the better in thoughts, behaviors, emotions and personality we call case gain (case: *the sum total of the person's non-optimum thoughts, disagreeable emotions and self-limiting behaviors*).

There are a number of signs that Hypnoetics™ is progressing nicely in the right direction. These are basically milestones of improvement and go as follows:

1. Willing to look at things
2. Willing to talk
3. Emerging rationality
4. New insights (*cognosis*)
5. Dropping away of the pain and negative
6. Positive feelings
7. Shift
8. Renewed abilities
9. Peak experiences

As a person progresses and gains increasingly correct perspectives on their inner domain, he or she will move through this hierarchy and it pays to be aware of it. Individual stages are discussed as follows:

1. The person has to be willing to talk freely about their life and experiences, otherwise, it's a no-go.

2. Emerging Rationality

The first change you will probably notice is they start to see things in a clearer, more logical way. Answers begin to make sense to YOU, as the pilot. The person starts to see WHY things have been the way they were. These self-observations have a kind of "rightness" that brings understanding and satisfaction.

Indeed, if this isn't happening, then something is wrong.

The fundamental process of piloting is the UNCOVERING of truth; we earlier called it unburdening. As the layers of illogicality and false emotion come away, the sense you are looking for should become clearer and clearer. Sometimes it happens in a flash; far more commonly, it is a gradual process.

Gradually, the client begins to see that the way he or she was thinking was stupid, illogical or destructive. But the emerging new version of circumstances, thoughts, beliefs or emotions makes more sense and is more empowering. This isn't a matter of the client making him or herself wrong; he or she becomes RIGHT by seeing something better. There may be a degree of negativity, it is true, from chagrin to embarrassment or misery, but it generally clears on inspection (remember the mechanics of Deep-IS, introduced on page 16).

The truth looks better and feels better than lies.

3. Cognosis (New Insights)

Cognosis is a process. As rationalization progresses, you will hear the client suddenly become aware of new dimensions and perspectives that liberate his or her thoughts and emotions. It is hard to describe this feeling, except by experiencing it. Fortunately, most of us do at some time or another.

Think of the last time you had a "Wow, now I can see why..." type of experience. Really, these sudden insights grow out of accumulated reason. As your client gains more understanding, he or she may come to see things in a completely new way and will not fall back to the old way of thinking.

4. Dropping Away of Pain and Confusion

You will observe that new awareness results in a freedom, a release from pain or unhappiness. The client felt bad about something; now he or she has grasped where it was all coming from and doesn't feel bad about it any more. He or she can "let go".

5. Positive Feelings or "Wins"

Next will come the surge of GOOD feelings. If (example) the client has felt depressed for years every time he or she looks in a mirror but now suddenly reports feeling great, then that is the emergence of great new emotions, such as happiness and delight, taking the place of the old gloom.

It's totally logical, actually.

6. Shift

In Supernoetics®, hence its baby-steps offshoot Hypnoetics™, we value shift. Most systems and "therapies" (like EFT) aim to see things differently from the same place. We want our clients to see things differently from a new place! Hence shift.

There will come times when he or she experience such a positive release that life changes forever at that moment. Feeling outrageously wonderful can and does happen with Punk Psychology™! People often liken it to floating on air; there is a definite sense of something have gone; dropped away.

Shift is not the act of getting rid of "stuff". Shift is what happens as *a result* of getting rid of stuff.

The way we see it in Supernoetics®, with educational programs and personal piloting, is that there are lots of "Aha!" moments, which build into shifts. Shift can come at you in spades or it can be gradual. We value it highly; the more of it the better!

That's how personal growth comes about; we improve how a person sees things; we improve abilities, attitudes and emotions; we handle (diminish) a person's case until he or she sheds unwanted layers of confusion, inability and compromise.

Hypnoetics™ is only the first stage of a whole range of techniques. We can truly boast in Supernoetics® we have "the protocols for change and human transformation™".

7. Renewed Abilities.

A major change in mental state will usually result in the recovery in some ability life. We speak often of negative gain, meaning inhibitors have vanished. The apparency of gaining something new is really the client re-discovering something about him or herself that was thought to have been lost. It was there all the time. Now it is free to express itself once more (akin to the somewhat disparaging phrase "born again").

Thus you may address all your negative thoughts about money to the point where you can suddenly deal with it in a new and remarkable way. Prosperity starts to happen for you. From struggle, you become a big-time money manager.

The point here is that rational action and rational thought are insepa-rable. If you are bugged by money handling (or whatever), it is because of disempowering beliefs, thoughts and emotions about money. If you can release those properly, then you will be able to act differently with money.

8. Peak Experiences

Finally, though sadly quite rare, you may experience one of those ec-static moments of sheer joy and beauty that Abram Maslow called "peak experiences". This is full of positive emotion and a bit like shift, but of a very different order of magnitude. The experience is so intense it takes on a semi-religious quality. People speak of universal love, an oceanic quality, out-of-body states, intensified perceptions, and indescribable beauty that is almost unbearable (Maslow, A. *Toward A Psychology Of Being*, New York: D. Van Nostrand Co., Second Edition, 1968).

Such events do occur spontaneously in people's lives, though there would typically be a triggering cause. Probably most people have them but these become so obscured by the dross of unpleasant experience that the majority of individuals cannot even remember being in such a state.

Piloting has the definite capability of delivering this condition to you, from time to time. It will generally happen as you progress, rather than early on. But there are no rules. It can burst upon you at any time.

Enjoy it for as long as it lasts. Link up to the rest of creation and enjoy the blissful feelings of being connected and serene. It is good to expe-rience our spiritual selves; such moments are precious and should be drunk to the full. Later we'll be sharing ways to make these states more accessible and more permanent.

Utilization

Use these positive signals to guide you deeper in regard to subjects being addressed. While it is going well in a particular direction, keep at it. The more transformation and benefit you can bring before switching the client to a new target area, the better. It would be a tactical error to give up or switch if good results are forthcoming. Yet many people do just that; be on guard against making this mistake yourself.

Renewed ability and feelings great about something is definitely the time to move on. You can work too much in an area if you allow yourself to become obsessed by it. Unfortunately, there is a gone-on-too-long factor, which can kick in and cause you trouble.

This "too much or too long" is another kind of untruth coming to cloud the situation. If you have dealt with the problem and got a result, to go on fussing at it is to state or imply that it has not been resolved, which is properly another kind of lie. Thus you will encounter more problems and difficulties.

Avoid it!

Punk Points:

- There are quite a few pointers to suggest a good time to end off, ranging from just sheer fatigue (which must be recognized), to blown-out excited. In neither state is a person really fit to be engaged with something new. Better to allow him or her rest for the former and time to come down to earth for the latter!

- Providing you are not running out on the client because things got tough, taking a break for any one of several reasons won't do any harm or stall the case.

- It is possible to identify a range of gradually expanding and improving states and abilities in a client, from being willing to take a look at things and start talking, through Aha! and cognosis moments, and shift, all the way up to what Abram Maslow called a "peak experience".

- If you later progress to learning the skills of using a GSR meter, you will find a number of other positive instrument responses that will also indicate to you that it's time to take a break for the present.

CHAPTER 16

MULTIPLE VIEWPOINT HYPNOETICS

You can extend the impact and power of Hypnoetics™ by a great deal if you will consider re-running key episodes from the viewpoint of other participants in the action. The trouble with a great deal of counseling, psychotherapy and PTSD handling is that they place the person firmly in a position of a victim. It's things "done to" him or her. Bad stuff; "You poor thing…"

Punk Psychology™ has a far higher level of view. We participate in our world in a way which offers few or no excuses.

The reality is we all participate in complex group dynamics or constellations (as covered in the *12 Channels Of Being*). By simply being there, we must accept some of the action as our own. Even babies, who you might think are innocent, are far more participative than they are given credit for. Once you accept the fact that we are born again and again, you will see that the child's journey through this life starts before he or she is even born. Being here on Earth at all is therefore a choice.

But for adults, the contribution to disruptive events is much clearer. The wife who drives her husband nuts, so he beats her; the husband who has affairs and drives his wife to distraction; teachers who provoke bad behavior in kids, and then punishes them; the boss who literally incites mutiny among his staff; the priest who molests little boys; and the crook who gets shot by his colleagues… these are all individuals who, in their way, are creating or participating in events going on around them.

The point is, they have their emotional charge too. It does not remain isolated however; not private and hidden. We can all sense each others' emotions. They impact us (think of a time when your lover or friend was down and remember how you felt as a result). It is then hardly surprising that the case in Hypnoetics™ can usefully process the charge of other individuals involved in the story.

You can almost predict it.

You can run a child's miserable life, because father was a bully and constantly beat the youngster. But then, if you turn it around, you can run the same story from the father's point of view. There is a lot of change to be had. Buckets of charge will come off on the GSR meter. But also the injured party (supposedly) will begin to see things about the father's life that mitigates the pain of his violence and cruelty.

Maybe father is just dramatizing what he had to endure as a child. This is the usual story, of course. Nobody is born evil. He or she is molded by experience and, since everyone is fairly inept at managing their case, parents are a most potent source of damaging actions and unwanted thoughts that a child picks up. Don't forget peers though; they have more effect than you would think.

Then we have wicked mothers who were, it turns out, thrashed and abused by Catholic nuns in the school where she was educated. Or the lover who was jilted wretchedly and who can now, no longer love in earnest. The flirt who was so crushed at school and in upbringing that he or she cannot feel loved and therefore cannot seriously love.

Once you see things from the other person's perspective, you start to have a great deal more compassion for their destructive dramas and emotional outbursts. In fact sometimes we find ourselves wondering how we would cope with the same circumstances.

A Sense Of Proportion

In Supernoetics® and baby-steps Hypnoetics™ we do not get heavy with responsibility; like Pohl Pot or Saddam Hussein were somehow your fault! Yes, we are all a part of the greater reality that we call our universe. We participate.

But to take on too much is to exaggerate responsibility and turn caring into pure burden and blame. We don't want that.

It's not helpful because we cannot influence events on the bigger scale—at least not *yet*.

There is a spiritual concept that we are responsible for everything. But even if true, this principle is so often misunderstood. It cannot be true from one single viewpoint, for example. If the Jews want to accept they were somehow responsible for the holocaust (what did the Jews do to cause this?), this cannot override the fact that Hitler has the main responsibility for the holocaust.

Yes, we have a degree of responsibility in all things but a sense of proportion is important. Otherwise we could start to accept that we are responsible for bad things done to us and nobody else is. The latter would be absurd.

So if the world ends due to a meteorite impact, we do not expect you to hold up your hands and say "Sorry folks!"

Conjoint Family Therapy

In Supernoetics® and Hypnoetics™ we greatly admire the pioneering work of Virginia Satir (1916-1988) and her Conjoint Family Therapy. Her model was that an individual's problems were inevitably bound up with the functioning of the group to which the person belonged; typically, the family (but not exclusively so).

It's a version of General Systems Theory, proposed by biologist Ludwig von Bertalanffy in 1928. Basically, Bertalanffy challenged the accepted idea that you could study something more closely by breaking it into parts and looking at the components. General Systems Theory says this is to miss the main point, which is that the whole is not just the sum of the parts; it's an entity in itself.

Satir's entire work was done under the umbrella of "Becoming More Fully Human". From the possibility of a nurturing primary triad of father, mother, and child she conceived a process of *Human Validation*. Her push towards world peace can be summed up in her own words:

"The family is a microcosm. By knowing how to heal the family, I know how to heal the world."

Today there is also Concurrent Therapy. With this approach the point is that the group is a separate entity, not just a composition of individuals. So therapy might be directed towards one of a pair, then the other of a pair and then finally *the pair as a duo*, a unity. The relationship itself is also a "case".

From these pioneer models we readily grasp that the simplistic "done to", or victim model, of most counseling and psychotherapy, is trivial and naïve to the point of being mostly worthless.

How Do We Use This?

The skilled Hypnoetics™ pilot, when encountering:

• A complex episode in which there are several players

• The events were turbulent and multifaceted

• And with heavy charge running (as shown by the GSR meter activity, if you are using one)...

will consider running the episode from the point of view of each of the other main participants.

If the child was being abused, run it from the abuser's point of view; if someone is seriously injured, run it from the point of view of the perpetrator; if there is oppression, borderlines in the picture, or [narcissists], run it from the wicked person's point of view. Perhaps he or she will not seem so wicked?

We have even successfully run Hypnoetics™ technique from the point of view of the airplane (feeling guilty) in a major crash. It's been done from God's point of view; or a fly on the wall! I suppose you could do it from the bed's point of view in a sordid extra-marital affair.

Truly, you can be as creative as you want, once you understand just what it means to "be" someone or something. French philosopher and vitalist Henri Bergson called it "sympathetic intelligence". We don't use that as a formal term in Supernoetics® but we fully embrace the concept and have pushed it far beyond anything that Bergson could have imagined!

The procedure is simple. There are no formalities or standard patter. Just announce: "We'll run this again, from the viewpoint of [other participant]." Make sure you orient to client to the correct point of view and he or she has grasped what that means.

Then, off you go:

"Move to the beginning of that episode..." etc.

He or she must speak as the person: "And then I hit her..." or whatever. NOT, "And then he hit me..." which would show the case was not occupying the correct viewpoint.

Other Aspects Of Running

The client may feel they have little awareness of what the other person could be thinking or feeling. Actually, they would be wrong. Such a client has just been conditioned to believe it's impossible to know. But if it makes him or her more comfortable, explain "We are just pretending". In any case, there are no right or wrong answers. This isn't a test to see if the client can guess correctly! It's just attempting to feel and think like the other person probably did.

Repeater can be useful: have the client say out loud any words used by the perpetrator or others involved. That helps to adopt his or her viewpoint.

Sensate awareness also works effectively. Whether it seems remarkable or not, our client can feel all the feelings of the other parties involved, their thoughts, emotions, bodily sensations and mental energies. Once you experience the phenomenon of interconnected consciousness, none of this is weird. It's obvious!

Any good pilot will tell you they feel with the client they are running, see his or her pictures, get the pain often before the client comments on it. This is all the same phenomenon at work.

It seems magic—and it is, within the idea of "magic"—but it's a scientific fact established by us in Supernoetics®.

This idea is now backed up by investigative brain scans. There is a phenomenon called "mirror neurons". When someone experiences pain, another person watching him or her will show activity in their brain scan that matches the scan of the person feeling the pain.

In fact this is scientific validation for universal consciousness, telepathy and telekinesis. However scientists miss that, poor things! But think about the implications...

Our Intuition

Children are very good at intuiting adult thoughts and feelings. To them it's natural. Their mirror neurons are probably lighting up like a Christmas tree all the time!

But it's drummed out of them. By the time they grow up, it has become a mechanical, impersonal world where scientists can seriously believe they are right when they dismiss telepathy, intuition and the like.

Probably the child's intuitive perception is the reason why so many children shoulder blame for what they see happening in the adult world around them. The can *feel* mother and father's frustration and anger at each other and so assume it's their frustration and anger too.

When there is an abuse case, the child can feel the lust and so blame themselves, because they find that feeling inside themselves, not "out there". The youngster may actually feel "dirty" and involved.

All this would be expected if our inter-personal constellation phenomenon is a real one. The child is in every sense a "part" of the whole and it is so very easy for them, in their naïve formative state, to take much of the blame. Indeed, unhappy and obnoxious adults are inclined, at times, to actually say to the child, "It's all your fault", meaning, if you hadn't been born your father and I would still be happy together.

Often true; but a thought that is utterly odious when put into words and spoken to a child.

Empowerment ··

Running as case as victim can eventually become disempowering. We don't go for very long in Hypnoetics™ before we need to change to positive and creative processing: learning to imagine and create things the way we want them, rather than the way the past just came at us. A later section in this book explains how to "re-write" a person's history; tell it anew, in a way which becomes thrilling and empowering, instead of demeaning and hurtful.

That's also the realm of revelation processing and advanced Supernoetics®. Hopefully you will move forward with us and aspire to this further training and research.

Meantime, we have to clear up some clutter, so we can get at our real mind, not just the reductionist, subconscious portion that keeps us ticking over. Multiple viewpoint running often represents a halfway stage to freedom. The person is victim and then is promoted to co-perpetrator. That's a significant improvement.

It is better to work the case as cause and responsibility. Even if we are not fully responsible for a crazy spouse, we are still totally responsible for our reactions to his or her antics.

However, with this new enlightened view, there is a third "presence" which is the conjoint partnership—the constellation. We are part of that too. We helped create it. We at least allowed it but—that's not strong enough—we helped create it the way it is because, at some level, that's what we wanted. Remember, everything has a context and you need to get down to that context before it starts to make sense.

Let's join Virginia Satir in the proud feeling that we know how to heal the world, starting with piloting, one individual at a time, then whole constellations.

Punk Points:

- The emotional "charge" and distress that we feel in unpleasant past encounters isn't all down to our own selfish hurts. Other people got caught up in this too and even the ones we elect as the one-and-only troublemakers have their own view of things. Almost nobody wants to be deliberately hurtful and destructive. We get into these binds through bad emotions, negativity and above all irrationality. We must shoulder our share in what has happened to us.

- We can actually process another party's point of view. We seem to know what he or she was really thinking and feeling. By running off their point of view, as well as our own, we gain insight and compassion. Forgiveness comes easy, once you realize the other person's motivation.

- This idea is now backed up by investigative brain scans. There is a phenomenon called "mirror neurons". When someone experiences pain, another person watching him or her will show activity in their brain scan that matches the scan of the person feeling the pain.

- The technique is very simple: have the client take up the other person's point of view and speak as if they were him or her. See and feel things how the other person would have experienced them.

- Virginia Satir was one of the first psychologists to point out that we are not single-entity persons. We are part of a group dynamic and all parts of that group interact. There is no "us and them" reality!

CHAPTER 17

THE COMPLEX OF SELF

Before we go on to new landscapes of the mind, let's get some additional context for what we are doing here. My own researches over the years have led me to the certain knowledge that thought is multi-dimensional and what we call "mind" has many layers or levels. We talk glibly of "mind, body and spirit" but it's surely even more subtle than that.

You need to be aware of the subtleties I will reveal below, because you will sometimes encounter them. Supernoetics® (and hence Hypnoetics™) are powerful vehicles of truth and sooner or later it all has to come tumbling out. You can run but you can't hide is a now-famous saying that could apply: no matter how you run to escape the truth within, you can't escape it!

This chapter will reveal aspects of your true nature you never knew.

At the top, of course, is consciousness. No arguments there. Consciousness to me is being there: *the awareness of being aware*. This is the highest state of our Being, or the expression of it.

Trouble is, it's rather hard to capture in words. Like the knife that cannot cut itself, words about consciousness are not really about consciousness but about a substitute precept. Real consciousness is actually an experience and cannot be captured in words. Hence the Zen metaphor of the finger pointing to the moon. The word "moon" is just a word, not an experience. All the talk does not capture what it means to be conscious and aware of being aware.

Consciousness as I define it here means awareness of awareness, thoughts about thinking, desires about desires, beliefs about beliefs. It has been called "the watcher"; the "witness"; it is seeing our self from on high. The viewpoint is looking down on the identity which it serves.

George Gurdjieff called this "self remembering". Really, you can't beat my expression, which says it all: *see yourself being yourself*. You watch the stream of your thoughts, emotions, efforts etc.

Modern hypnotism researchers, notably Ernest Hilgard, have developed what they call the "hidden observer" idea. This higher, more intelligent, more aware and discerning version of consciousness can maintain a degree of outside objectivity, no matter the depth of trance. It is still sufficiently independent to be able to identify and discard what is offensive, irrelevant or disempowering.

In piloting it is important that we train our clients to be able to see themselves from "on high", looking down from what I call the glass elevator. There are several "floors" to this elevator and we need to be adept at stepping from floor to floor.

Let's start at the bottom and work up...

The Brain

Here is the animal or physical level of thinking. This is brain stuff. Some of it is reflex and instinctual. But it's a broader concept than that, meaning the animal part of us, or what I call "creature", has its own agenda and it has nothing to do with spirituality or purpose. In fact it's all about staying alive: eating, safety, procreation and very little else.

I'm not just referring to what's sometimes called the "lizard brain". Cognitive functioning is there, but only in a very primitive, unaware state. This is the typical modern human being—cell phone clapped to the ear; seeing, hearing and believing that reality is only what comes in through the biological sense organs. We call this person the "IS-person" and the reality they experience has dwindled down to what we call Simple-IS: what you see is what you get and that's all there is and all there ever will be.

Sad!

As I often point out, most of the confusion in physiology, psychology and philosophy comes from the failure to recognize we are entities in two modes: the spirit being and the biological creature. These two halves do not readily reconcile and harmonize; in fact they are often in direct conflict.

Thus the Catholic priest, supposedly celibate, who ends up molesting young kids. His creature half starts to over-ride his spiritual half and tragedy is the result (comes from setting impossible spiritual goals, which fail to take account of the fact that we are all biological creatures).

In my view, the single biggest confusion in psychology and spiritual practices is the failure to distinguish the different modalities and goals that characterize our creature side from those which are spiritual purposes aspirations.

The creature and spirit are not only different in nature; *they are often heavily in conflict with each other*. For some great reading, check out Melvin Konnor's very capable book *The Tangled Wing*. The latest editions have been much enhanced with data and are becoming compendious; but Konnor's basic premise—that our biological imperatives stand in the way of our spiritual life and, in many cases, completely trounce and entangle it—remains unchanged.

I see this important point missed time and time again, as people struggle with physical infirmity, while they try to "go spiritual" or who curse and punish themselves for manifesting what are perfectly valid creature needs (like eating and sex). If you have creature issues, they will stand in your way until you resolve them. Just trying to pretend they will go away is a poor approach to truth.

Remember: the creature has memory too. It has mind and Being. We call that the protoplasm entity (chapter 17).

Neural Nets

Rising out of brain physiology is the concept of neural networks. These are different to, and somewhat more sophisticated than, purely brain-based reflexes and reactions. This is a level of thought experience that is partly biological but not entirely. By that I mean there is a physical element but also an energetic aspect.

There is reason to believe that such networks are far greater than the boundaries of the brain itself. Indeed, we now talk of the "gut brain", meaning the nerve plexus system found in the gut. It has as many neurones as the brain and in fact carries over 80% of the body's "happy hormone" serotonin.

Neural nets are self-organizing and to a degree self-aware. They can learn and self-correct. In other words, neural nets too have memory. The neural nets are almost an entity of self... almost but not quite.

When you consider the effect of brain stimulation, through drugs, entrainment devices and so on, it's obvious there is an important layer of conscious thought experience sandwiched between spirit and the body mind. It can be manipulated, changed, or overridden but it's there.

It particularly stands out to me in the matter of sex. The arousal of heart and mind while making love to that special partner has strongly physical elements, as we all know. But there is definitely a higher process, in the way one's brain activity changes. In fact changes in consciousness run all the way up to the spiritual during sex, as many of us know.

Sex is capable of changing one's entire thought landscape, at least short-term. How long that interval is depends on the relationship but, as I wrote in my tender piece "Waves That Thrill", the slow build up of rapport can take place over days before the actual act and the sighing echoes of it can linger and slowly dissipate for days afterwards.

A lot of recent science has gone into studying neural networks; they are very cunning and able to self-reference and learn. We now have non-biological neural networks that are, in effect, electronic bots. In fact smartphones wouldn't work without them. The thing is, they don't need fully programming. They only have to be set up to learn... and they do!

Certainly the smartphone is an extension of memory, perception and thought. It is, in every sense, an extension of self and that's important enough to incorporate in any system of psychology.

Neural nets can mimic many functions of the human mind but are not (so far) conscious in the sense we would mean it. Machines will become vastly intelligent, but they're still lacking this sense of being in the world.

A word of caution: orthodox religions (and cults) use cynical neural network training (indoctrination). They are nowhere close to the level of thought and spirit, to which they lay claim.

Action and Intention ···

Next floor: behaviors. What we do in action is a species of thinking! This is the basic manifestation of ideas and intention. J F Skinner thought (or wrote) that behaviors are all there is to thinking. He called the mind a "convenient fiction". A whole psychological movement was founded on this strange concept, called behaviorism.

Of course what we mainly see about a person is what they are actually doing and we all know that's often very different to what the person is saying, or thinking. Behavior will disclose thinking to a degree but it is not always possible to accurately know what a person is thinking from his or her behaviors.

Intention is important here because there is a level of action which comes at the psychic level. A person can *intend* certain things, meaning they apply force or action at the psychic level. It's kind of inward action. We may see nothing outwardly but the person is putting a great deal of "creative pressure" on the outcome.

In everyday terms it's what we call a wish or desire. Affirmations are an attempt to use the power of thought and intention to get what you want.

It can have many layers of subtle interaction between people, beings and entities. We may intend a person to depart or intend (wish) him or her to fall in love with us. These are perfectly valid actions or behaviors when it comes to piloting. Indeed, it could be said that this level of "thinking", action and energy is the most important aspect of past experiences which have lingered to haunt and hurt us. We have a special technique for clearing them from a case called Transformational Mind Dynamics™ or TMD.

This was developed for us by Heidrun Beer and Rolf Dane in Copenhagen, Denmark, and hence are jokingly referred to as the "Copenhagen Codes". We teach this technique to professionals.

Emotions

Next in my mind hierarchy is emotions. I think it is a definite level of conscious experience, a level of thinking, and considering the vast majority of people never rise much above this level, it needs clearly recognizing for what it is.

People identify so completely with their complex emotional world that the usual manner of speech is to say "I AM happy", as if happy was the self; I AM angry or I AM sad, or you ARE antagonistic.

In actuality it would be better to say, "I am doing happiness" or "I am doing anger" because that's the truth of emotions: we generate them ourselves, in order to experience them.

It's absurd to say to someone "You upset me" or "You make me angry". You do it to yourself and then (usually) complain about it!

Of course not all emotions are negative, though that's usually what people mean by the word. But don't forget the positive emotions, which can be thrilling indeed: joy, The Flow, bliss and excitement are just a selection of the available positive emotions.

A key point to remember about emotions is that they are at the point of transition between physical biology and non-material thought. Emotions are stimulated by insubstantial ideas in the mind, but they manifest physically and you can see emotions; even feel them when in a person's presence.

Thought

Above emotion comes thought. Thoughts and concepts include perceptions and experiences and give rise to the illusion of being a separate identity. This is where words come in: concepts and ideas. Words verbalize our thoughts. Thoughts actually create and monitor our experiences. If you think your life isn't so good, think a different thought, "My life is great!" and it all changes.

It's true that our experience of reality is entirely dictated by how we respond to events. We create our experience from the inside out and we are not really the victim of outside events (unless we make conscious choice to be a victim of outside events!) Most people do make that choice but it's a simple switch to stop it: change your thinking. *A better version of reality is just one thought away.*

Talking of concepts creating our reality; this is the realm of so-called beliefs. Beliefs are not ingrained or unalterable and cannot be blamed on spirit. Beliefs are simply a response to experience. Beliefs are largely conditioned, and that's the truth.

Thought, of course, conjures up the concept of mind. In Supernoetics® we recognize the extended mind concept: the mind is not confined to the brain. The mind extends outwards infinitely in all directions. This is written up elsewhere.

The Cell Phone Metaphor

Take out your cell phone and look at it. With that small hand-held device, you can call anywhere on Earth: New York, London, Moscow, Sydney, Delhi. Does that mean all those cities exist inside your cell phone? Of course not. But that's the stupid logic of science: because we reach out to our thoughts and emotions, via the brain, therefore everything we think and feel comes from the brain!

Part of the proof is supposed to be that if you tweak certain parts of the brain, the messages we receive are distorted. Therefore the brain must be the origin of all messages. But if you stick a screwdriver in the back of your cell phone, you are going to garble the messages, or even lose them altogether.

Does that prove that New York and the rest of the world are in your cell phone?

We can access the Internet via a smartphone. The Internet is no more inside the phone than thoughts and emotions are inside the brain!

The current theory is too stupid to waste any more time on.

The Morphic Learning Field •••••••••••••••••••••••••••••••••••••••

You might think some of this is a bit far-fetched. But in fact there is wonderful emergent science in this field. None is more powerful than Rupert Sheldrake's model of a morphic field and the phenomenon of morphic resonance. It's a whole new take on thinking and learning.

Sheldrake is a mainstream scientist, with an interest in neglected or so-called paranormal phenomena. He has accrued scientifically valid data to show that we can tell when we are being stared at from behind; the we can know in advance when someone is going to call us on the phone; and that dogs (as well as other animals) do truly know when their master is coming home.

The point is, obviously, that there is no way such phenomena could occur within the accepted "laws" of physics.

But Sheldrake's most pivotal experiments were to do with learning. Experimental animals were placed under conditions in which they learn to respond to a given stimulus in a characteristic way. They are then made to repeat this pattern of behavior many times. According to the theory of morphic resonance, subsequent animals, even without being trained, ought to be able to access the field and benefit from the learning of previous animals. And that's exactly what he found.

All steps were taken to make sure there was no genetic transference of knowledge (not possible on the current "scientific" model, anyway) or learning indirectly or through observation. Sheldrake concluded that later generations of animals learned from some kind of generalized non-material memory field.

In fact this morphic resonance field became so powerful that subsequent animals made no mistakes whatsoever.

Perhaps this could be the beginning of the interconnectivity we consider the Divine element?

100 Monkeys

This famous application of the morphic resonance field, started, I think, with Lyall Watson in his marvelous book *Lifetide* (Hodder and Stoughton, London, 1979, pp. 174-177). The observations around which it is based have been subsequently denied by the Japanese researchers but that may be expediency or fear of being drawn in to New Age thinking! Whatever, the model is here to stay, largely because most of us have experienced some degree of its working.

What supposedly happened is that a young female macaque monkey called Imo learned to wash potatoes before eating them. Slowly the skill was passed around the colony, the adults learning from this youngster, by observation and mimicking. When a sort of critical mass number of monkeys had cottoned on to the trick, it suddenly spread like wildfire around neighboring islands and to mainland troops of monkeys, without any means of direct communication.

Now the term "one hundred monkeys" has entered the language, to mean exactly what Lyall Watson described: that when a sufficient number of individuals get on the same wavelength or behavior, unified thinking starts to spread outwards, with a momentum of its own, seemingly carried along by a non-material field or connectivity of some kind.

This is probably the reason that discoveries seem to come in rushes. Someone, somewhere, gets and idea and all of a sudden, at around the same time, several totally independent thinkers come up with the same idea: for example, calculus was discovered by Sir Isaac Newton, and very closely afterwards by Liebniz, who had no communication of any kind with Newton.

The spread of knowledge becomes an unstoppable force or wave. In the words of Victor Hugo, *nothing is as powerful as an idea whose time has come.*

OK, moving on up...

Just Knowing ··

There is a level of thought and awareness here, waiting to be fully explored. It is characterized by non-verbal knowing. We can sense it, indulge it, experience it. But it's impossible to define in any meaningful sense.

Hence the Zen metaphor of a finger pointing to the moon referred to above.

This level of knowing gives rise to many transcendent, non-material and trans-personal phenomena, such as intuition, prescience, telepathy and telekinesis.

Some people manifest considerable abilities at this level Most often it is a barely controlled and improperly understood phenomenon but it nevertheless real. As I said, it needs much more exploration. But just to put it there, on the map for all to see, is a strong statement of consciousness, awareness and knowing!

In 1961, science fiction writer Robert Heinlein, in his book *Stranger In A Strange Land*, had his Martian guy Valentine Michael Smith able to just "grok" things. I remember at the time we youngsters took to this word and used it frequently. It seemed to fill a gap where there was no real word for such a specific phenomenon.

You will begin to encounter this deeper non-verbal knowing, even at the simple level of Hypnoetics™ procedures. It is a species of truth and truth is what we release from the cage, when doing Hypnoetics™ piloting!

It is so much more exciting than the made-to-think levels of social enforcement, collective mind, memes and education!

Cloud Consciousness ··

You might suppose we are already considerably into the woo-woo land of mysticism and magic! But from here on up, things get mighty interesting. Another level of consciousness suggests itself, which I have labeled the "Self-Complex". This needs explaining. Basically, we are not—at least not initially—a single conscious unity. We are a cloud of consciousness entities, operating within the same psychic space.

This might sound strange to you at first but actually this concept is present in our everyday language, once you know what to look for. Common expressions that represent this phenomenon include: "I'm of two minds about this." "Something tells me...," "My gut tells me...," "A little voice inside whispered to me..."

Some these beings we share with are, in effect, multiple parts of the self ("other selves"), whereas some are present, definitely creating an influence, but *not part of self*, so I would call these "non-self others". This concept extends to include the phenomenon of so-called "entities" or walk-ins and is explained in more detail in later materials.

What we believe to be our "self" is in fact a conglomerate of individual viewpoints, with varying degrees of penetration and expression in the individual's personality. Sometimes a wholly different viewpoint may take over, as with a serial killer, many of who claim no knowledge of what the evil part has done.

Eventually the true Executive Self will re-assert its authority. But it is by no means as simple as Freud and later psychologists thought. It has been stated we are a "mob"! This is true, at least up to the point where we start shedding these extra consciousness particles, in the Extreme Mysticism levels of Supernoetics®.

I'm talking about what Buddha called the "fleas". Other writers have written about being taken over or occupied by a so-called "entity". This is slightly different. What I am talking about is really like a composite consciousness, rather than being taken over by an invader.

Of course the average person is totally unaware that his or her mind is actually divided into multiple entities, capable of acting independently. The reason is that in most people, these parts of self are so well integrated that we rarely notice when control shifts from one to another.

The illusion of a single mind is further enhanced by the fact that all the multiple consciousness particles are associated with the same body and thus the same name; each one considers itself to be "I". The "I's" are most noticeable when they are in conflict with each other. We then have "mixed feelings": coexisting contrary attitudes.

A particularly brilliant model in this respect is Dick Schwartz's Internal Family Systems. He's not talking about family in the normal sense, but the family of selves within.

Of course there is a kind of "executive self", one who rides over and above all, looking, thinking, sensing and above all Being, as a single-focus viewpoint. That could be called the True Self. As we progress along our spiritual pathway, shedding unwanted encumbrances and identities, we come closer and closer to our pure Self or Being.

But the final stages of the path are to surrender our individual ego or Being altogether. We join with the God layer, which will be described shortly. A lot of people don't want to surrender the Self; the idea frightens them. Of course it is not necessary to return to the God state. It's a choice.

The Fourth Way (Self-Remembering)

Gurdjieff was particularly insightful on this aspect of multiple consciousness. His famous "Fourth Way" was about trying to disentangle one's True Self from this net of other selves or "I"s. Gurdjieff thought you could master this phenomenon by just observing it carefully and becoming aware of what was going on. However I have found it is way beyond most people's ability to get to grips with.

Fortunately, we have our Golden Path, which leads the individual, step by guided step, into higher levels of ability and awareness. We learn to crawl, then walk, then run and then... fly!

You may need to start disentangling the Self and working with your separate parts at the very start, while doing the early steps. But that's rare. Usually, the awareness required to start shedding the Complex of Self comes later along The Golden Path. Still, it gives you an insight into what it means, to be a multiple Self. What you supposed were fixed thoughts, patterns or intrusive behaviors may turn out to be other parts of you, or even other beings from this Cloud Consciousness. It's a fascinating road to self-discovery.

When you know what to do, it isn't difficult or dangerous. But you need the telepathic ability and the verbal skills to deal with most of these strange beings.

For the protection of every individual, these materials remain confidential, until you are ready.

God-ness and Separation

God. Just for once, I'm going to tackle this loaded "God" concept, at least in principle. I have no wish to intrude on anyone's beliefs. But the first thing to state is that a "god" who is on the same emotional level as us (with a vengeful, misogynistic attitude and anger management issues) doesn't make any sense. There has to be something higher than that.

What we in Supernoetics® consider the equivalent of God is in fact a *state of Being*. We could call it the "God structure". It's the highest level of awareness and has no separate Self! God isn't, and cannot be, separate from our selves.

To me, talk of a separate God comes only from fools who don't understand their own language. There is no logical, semantic or experiential reality in trying to create a separated "God". Universal consciousness, which we may elect as the creator of real and physical things, is infinite in all aspects. It is present everywhere and in all things. It is everything people ascribe to a divine God.

In the deepest depths of time, when we found a way to separate, we began dropping down from the infinite knowing, loving and aware state, to become a "Self". But although the Self is aware (self-aware), it is not fully developed consciousness. We have surrendered some of that infinite vastness, for the experience of separate Being.

We now have a separate viewpoint. But God occupies all viewpoints; hence is immanent in all things.

In Ascension, which is the reverse of individuation, the more conscious you become, the more your sense of Self fades; the more you join with God, the more you lose identity. And that's a universal, by the way, found in all writings from all spiritual sources.

Love becomes inevitable. It is a core teaching of Supernoetics® that we *are* love. Love is not something we give or get; it is not even something we do; love is *what we are*. It is our nature.

Probably this, more than anything I can think of, gave rise to the saying that "God is love".

Let's just leave it at that.

The Glass Elevator Model

Personal coach Michael Neill introduced me to a useful techno-metaphor; that of the glass elevator. It starts on the ground floor, with just the basic, unrefined view of things, which is what we experience and believe to be true. Simple-IS, we call it.

But as this glass elevator starts to climb, we gain a higher and higher viewpoint, seeing more and more how our thoughts determine emotions and experience; thoughts actually create our own reality. Until at the top floor level, it becomes obvious to us that what we experience depends entirely on our choice of what we want to experience.

All the "law of attraction" phoney-baloney taps into this concept, which is that thoughts create our world. What the wannabe gurus forget is that you have to have the elevator! You can't fly in at the top floor level and that's the uncomfortable truth!

Here's the elevator ride as I have stated it (this time top to bottom):

- Universal Consciousness (oneness of all)
- Own Consciousness (executive self)
- The Self-Complex
- Knowing and Intuition
- Collective think (morphic resonance)
- Thought (mind)
- Emotion (mind and body)
- Action and Intention (Behaviors, doing)
- Neural-Network (special case)

- Animal (physical-physiological)

Always strive to go higher and higher. Try to see the world from a viewpoint above the one you are currently occupying and you will soon see that, as if by magic, your experience of reality gets better and wiser.

Punk Points: ••

- Layers of thought are far more complex than psychologists and scientists have ever understood. Our body (the "creature") gives rise to a whole range of thoughts; at the opposite end is the sublime and infinite spiritual being.

- Thought, emotion and behaviors are familiar levels of thinking (behaviors imply thought). But it is very clear we are majorly influenced by the thoughts of others: "collective think" as we call it. Rupert Sheldrake has also taught us about morphic resonance fields which are learning fields. Fields are everywhere (no holes, no gaps) and extend to infinity. Something "uploaded" to the morphic resonance field can be downloaded by anyone, anywhere, at any time. Maybe this is the origin of the myth of the "Akashic Records".

- Above the everyday recognized thought is a level of non-verbal knowing. We just "get it". In his 1961 book *Stranger In A Strange Land*, writer Robert Heinlein had his Martian guy Valentine Michael Smith able to just "grok" things. It's a tempting word and covers the case very nicely!

- The Tangled Wing is a useful term to highlight the difficulty of living as both a spiritual entity and a flesh body. The conflicts between the two are at times irreconcilable and the material body does seem to often clip our wings and stop us taking to the air as free-flying spirits!

CHAPTER 18

THE TRUTH ABOUT PAST LIVES

Belief in reincarnation allows you to experience history as yours. It gives you a different sense of what it means to be human.
— Dr. Paul DeBell, Cornell-trained psychiatrist

In our quest for rationality, truth and Being, there is one important question to be examined and discussed: the matter of reincarnation.

Like it or not; believe in reincarnation or not; you will come up against this phenomenon in Hypnoetics™. Religious people have been indoctrinated that there is no such thing. Dr. Ian Stevenson MD collected two whole volumes of cases, documenting their details and in many cases following up to check they were "real" (see below).

Even Freud did not accept this idea, though his mentor Janet clearly describes it. In his book *The Interpretation of Dreams*, Freud gives a clear description of a past life memory—related below—but he dismisses it as just a dream.

Personally, to me the weird idea is that you only live once and then "die". If consciousness is a non-material phenomenon, that means it has no time and space; in other words it's timeless; in other words, it's never ending. Consciousness cannot die. Therefore it must move on.

Wherever you stand, you must not let your own prejudices enter. People are entitled to believe their own memories and think what they like about life and death.

The truth is: if you don't want to encounter past lives, keep clear of Punk Psychology™! Sooner or later in piloting, memories will surface, indistinguishable in quality from recalling your breakfast yesterday, which are clearly from other incarnations.

Not Sure?

Let me tell you about the work of Arnall Bloxham. He was a hypnotist working on past lives in the 60s and 70s. He did a series of cases that were shown on BBC2. The most outstanding story was about a woman who remembered a life as a young Jewess in York around 1194. She remembered so much detail they had to have a professor of medieval history verify that what she was describing was true for the time, which it was. There was a pogrom and she remembered being murdered in a crypt in St Mary's Church, with her two children. I know the very church, I'm very fond of York.

It was a moving story but the problem was there was nothing to back it up. Unfortunately, there was no such crypt. That is, there wasn't at the time of the broadcast... When this got really electric was, in fact some 10 years later, when the very crypt she described came to light. It has been buried for over 700 years. There was no way she could have known of the existence of that crypt in this life; *nobody knew* it was there.

The question is, how could she know about this crypt? What explanation is there for this memory? As I see it, you have two choices. It was either a weird, weird, weird coincidence—the kind scientists invoke to escape threats to their dogmas and theories. Or it was a true memory. I think it is much simpler to say, there are past lives. Now if one case isn't enough for you, there are now hundreds of these stories with this sort of circumstantial back up.

The Dogon People

Here is some more interesting detail, this time from an African tribe, the Dogon people from Mali. Their religion is all about the fact that they worship a minor companion to the star called Sirius, also known as the Dog Star. It's the brightest star in the northern sky, near the constellation of Orion (the one with 3 stars forming a belt).

This African tribe, and I'm talking about black people who live in mud huts, have a whole system of worship based on the companion to this star, called Sirius-B. They've been doing that for centuries. The only trouble is that science didn't discover the existence of this second star till a few decades ago. How did these simple people know that companion star was there? It's been christened the *Sirius Mystery*. Actually, it's very simple – the Dogons had some past lives there. They are just remembering it. Either there is some very very weird humbug or coincidence explanation, typical of the doubters and narrow-minded naysayers, or these people have actually been there and they are today congregating in Africa, just remembering the old times!

Discoveries like these make it seem impossible NOT to believe that people are remembering some earlier incarnation.

I come to the key question I want to challenge you all with. It's this: if we have lived before, we live over and over, we're immortal! If past lives are true and we keep on living, where the hell have we been until now? There are huge, huge acres of time we need to fill. Where were we?

Silver Space Ships

It turns out that people have incredibly clear memories of other worlds, other creatures, other realities, other times. Some of these alien societies are truly what have been christened "extra-terrestrial", which means capable of travel between worlds. Memories of silver space ships and the like are far from rare.

In fact I have long speculated that so-called science fiction works (like Jules Verne, Arthur C. Clark and Frank Herbert) are really just memory-derived stories from authors with a particular kind of bent for remembering other, alien planets. In other words, it's not really fiction!

Science readily admits that there are plenty of habitable worlds out there. Mathematical probability puts the numbers into the billions. We have been cruising the highways of the Cosmos for a very long time. It's not just about Earth and its environs. Some beings even have memories of what you could call "other universes", especially using theta brainwave devices. These machines can deliver an experience equivalent to decades of Buddhist meditation techniques.

We also meet people in life sometimes who are very "other worldly". Just be aware that he or she may truly be from another world and not quite fitting into ours. Children, for example, very dreamy and not quite "with it" are often stuck in earlier incarnations, in a different time and place.

Some people (I'm one) can remember thousands of past lives, just as clearly and with the same *quality* of memory that I can remember my childhood days.

Thing is, if you question dates ("How long ago was this?") you get some amazing answers, from millions or billions, trillions to quadrillions of years ago. Yes, all this is supposed to be before the start of the physical universe (the Big Bang). It's important to understand that science has not the faintest idea when this universe began. Their theories have fallen apart on all sides and I would quietly forget the off-the-wall estimate of 13 billion years, if I were you.

I trust the metered response from one of our psychonauts on the track of truth more readily than I trust some silly science speculations that have been advanced to the status of a theory. Three reasons:

1. Science is notoriously bad on this and not to be trusted

2. People get well and recover remarkable psychic abilities (remote viewing, telekinesis, telepathy, etc.) by accepting their own truth, as superior to "science".

3. The presence of other beings in the overwhelming vastness of space and the deeps of time seems more natural and obvious than just us being here.

Want Some More Science?

Remember a young child may have just died. He or she may be very upset. Dr. Ian Stevenson (1918 – 2007) from The Division of Perceptual Studies (DOPS) at the University of Virginia's School of Medicine collected two volumes of fully-authenticated cases of childhood remembrances of previous incarnations. They really stack up.

A colleague of Stevenson's at DOPS, Dr. Jim Tucker, a Bonner-Lowry Associate Professor of Psychiatry and Neurobehavioral Sciences, with a bachelor's degree from the University of North Carolina at Chapel Hill, and an M.D. from the University of North Carolina School of Medicine, describes the case of a two year old boy, James Leininger, from Louisiana, who reported memories of flying a fighter in World War II.

At around age 2, James Leininger experienced terrible nightmares, almost nightly, of violent plane crashes. During the day, he relayed extremely vivid memories of this supposed Air Force career. He recalled the name of a real aircraft carrier stationed in the Pacific during World War II ("Natoma"). He claimed to have a friend on the ship named Jack Larsen. James had memory of being shot down by the Japanese and dying near Iwo Jima.

The USS *Natoma Bay* lost only one pilot at Iwo Jima, a man named James Huston, and he died in a crash that matched Leininger's description almost exactly.

It's hard to say how Leininger or his parents might have known anything about James Huston before the nightmares began. How could a two-year old have gained or manufactured such knowledge, other than the simple and obvious explanation: he was remembering?

I no longer feel any drive to authenticate past life memories. It's not necessary. If just one is true, they could all be. There are even idiots who reason that if you can discredit one story, you have discredited them all. Logically, it's the other way round. Just one documented and proven story has to have a full explanation. It can't be shrugged off.

Of course there are card-carrying skeptics. There always will be. As Ian Stevenson has said: "The wish not to believe can influence as strongly as the wish to believe." It's just that skeptics are not usually honest enough to admit their own prejudices.

"I'm happy to say [Stevenson's work is] all complete and utter nonsense," wrote psychologist Jesse Bering in *Scientific American*. Actually, he was being ironic! He tended towards the opposite view: "The trouble is, it's not entirely apparent to me that it is [nonsense]. So why aren't scientists taking Stevenson's data more seriously?"

The information being collected at DOPS is certainly unusual. But overall, the organization functions no differently than any other scientific research outfit. Under Dr. Jim Tucker, strict adherence to scientific method laid down by the late Dr. Stevenson is still firmly in place. And according to Tucker, the essential motivation of scientists at DOPS is the same as that at NASA, WHO, and other institutions devoted to scientific inquiry: "We're just trying to find the truth."

Freud and Past Lives

Freud never mentioned or wrote about past lives. He called death "the aim of all life".

However I found a patient's account of what was clearly a past life in his book *The Interpretation of Dreams*, but unacknowledged as such by Freud:

On account of something or other that is happening in Rome it is necessary for the children to flee, and this they do. The scene is then laid before a gate, a double gate in the ancient style (the *Porta Romana* in Siena). I am sitting on the edge of a well, and I am greatly depressed; I am almost weeping. A woman—a nurse, a nun—brings out the two boys and hands them over to their father, who is not myself. The elder is distinctly my eldest son, but I do not see the face of the other boy. The woman asks the eldest boy for a parting kiss...

The "dream" apparently was triggered by watching a play *The New Ghetto*. In Hypnoetics™ we would say that play reconsolidated the past life memory, which came vividly into consciousness that night. Calling it a dream, of course, corrupts the memory because it is a false evaluation. That makes it stick.

In modern times, an American hypnotherapist called Morey Bernstein brought the therapy back to life in 1960's when he published *The Search For Bridie Murphy*, an account of one of his clients who went back over two hundred years, to when she was an Irishwoman called Bridie Murphy.

Dr. Brian Weiss published *Many Lives, Many Masters* in 1988. In that book he details his work with a patient he calls Catherine, who, under hypnosis, remembered multiple past lives, relieving her of paralyzing phobias. It has sold more than a million copies.

At the time he was heavily censured by colleagues but today, says Weiss, "Doctors are e-mailing me. They're not so concerned with their reputations and careers. We can talk about this openly. And it's not just psychiatrists, but surgeons and architects."

It's Commoner Than You Think ···

The reason most people are not directly in contact with their own memories of earlier incarnations is that they believe they will live only once. It's doctrinaire and forced on people by the priest classes, who don't want anyone to have any mode of escape from their thralldom. You can see why the rulers don't like the reincarnation concept and edited it out of *The Bible*: if people really do live over and over, you can't enslave them. More importantly, you can't even scare them with your bully tactics and false stories about "eternal torment" in the after life.

The Essenes knew all about re-incarnation. I'm not a Christian scholar but since we are powerfully influenced by Christian principles in the West, it's worth pointing out that in *The Gospel Of The Holy Twelve*, Jesus is said to have taught that souls reincarnate in order to gain experience in their quest for perfection. "The soul is purified through many births and experiences," says the deleted scripture.

The famous Cathars, a Christian sect which flourished in parts of southern France and northern Italy in the 12th and 13th Centuries, also believed in reincarnation. That was unacceptable to the then-Pope (Innocent III), who had every last one of them... men, women and children, slaughtered without mercy. It was one of the most ghastly massacres of all time, running to the tens of thousands of innocent victims—all killed with malice-aforethought by the official Church. That's how much religious authorities dread the truth about past lives.

Not all religions, of course. Gadadhara Pandit Dasa, Columbia University's first Hindu chaplain, calls reincarnation "a re-do," like a test you get to take over. After an unspecified number of tries, the eternal soul finally achieves some version of perfection. Only then, in what Hindus call *moksha* (or release), does the soul go to live with God.

Buddhists, it is well-known, steadfastly believe in reincarnation and also see it as a means of growth, learning and purification. There are some stupid notions abounding in this venerable religion, such as the idea we start as a beetle or worm and work our way up through the animal kingdom. In truth we all start as part of the God Structure and it's downhill from there!

The thing is, Buddhists make little or no attempt to remember earlier incarnations.

In Supernoetics® (and hence Hypnoetics™) we consider it essential to get to these earlier pivotal incarnations. They are there, fore sure, and sooner or later will rise, unprompted, to the surface.

New Age Follies

Modern bunglesome exponents, who plunge people into unnecessary and distressing memories, are mostly showing off. The worst proponent of all is the smarty-pants New Age therapist who claims the right and the ability to tell people what lives they have lived before.

This is not only a gross infringement; it's stupid, rude and likely to lead to harm. Most often it's the "therapist" dumping their own stuff on the client. I consider it a demonic practice to do this.

We, on the other hand, never tell people what to think in Hypnoetics™. We want the client to work it out for him- or her self. That way is empowering. Having some goosy woman crank telling you what she thinks happened to you is to disempower you and diminish your Beingness.

Bad.

Marooning someone in a past life is another folly I have seen on occasion. People who are less than capable hypnotists and other psychotherapists will oftentimes take a person back into an earlier incarnation memory, get excited, drool and cluck over it, then come back to present time. "There, you see?" he or she says, triumphantly.

But the incident is left un-discharged (not flattened properly) and so can lead to a bad re-load of a heavy memoneme which contains violence, brutality and very unpleasant physical sensations. There may be nightmares and sickness to follow, like Freud's case, described above, as a direct result of triggering something which is then left "live".

In Hypnoetics™ procedure, as in all Supernoetics® piloting, we flatten what we find as we go, discharging all MIMPs of their force. That way the person is released from the clutches of past events, not anchored to them.

Flattening as We Go

This concept of reducing or "flattening" what we find is crucial. It requires the pilot or exponent to rise above timidity. It can be very repetitious and somewhat counter-intuitive. The secret is to keep going, past all negative emotions, beyond boredom and into a cheerful re-evaluation of the past.

Finding and unburdening "earlier related" memories, Freud style, is part of this flattening process. If the memory you are running is dull and lifeless, the chances are there is something earlier to address.

It's a major skill to spot when to go earlier, without abandoning the current episode while it is still worth working on. If in doubt, give a few more passes to the one you are on. All of us pilots know moments when something appeared to be going on too long, when suddenly—like turning on a light switch—the client burst into laughter and sudden new insights, entering what we call a process of *cognosis*.

As you read in chapter 16, further unburdening comes about when we run the points of view of other people involved in the episode in question.

Now remember, just because an episode goes flat for one day, doesn't mean it could not be alive again, in the right circumstances. If there is no further change after several passes through, the episode is flattened *for that day*. But you could check it tomorrow, find it is still charged and run it some more.

Chapter 13 gives more details on the right choices for the moment to quit.

Always check that, unless it is very clear that this episode is GONE... gales of laughter, new abilities surfaced, couldn't find anything negative, even by trying, and it's vanished from view.

Punk Points:

- Whether you accept such a phenomenon or not, past life memories will come up. It's not your place to cast doubt on the meaning of such memories. To do so would be an act of pure psychic malevolence towards anyone you are supposedly trying to help.

- In fact there is abundant evidence for re-incarnation. The weird view is that we only live once. If we truly are non-material consciousness, our core being is timeless as well as without substance. It cannot die. Consciousness persists forever. The interesting question then arises: where have we been for all eternity, till now?

- All you need to concern yourself about in piloting is that these memories process exactly the same as this-lifetime memories. Past life events are, typically, more violent and therefore more likely to persist as memonemes.

- Getting the charge off such powerful and violent memories (often scenes of death) is very good for a case.

CHAPTER 19

RE-WRITING PERSONAL HISTORY

In Supernoetics® we boast "The Protocols Of Change and Human Trans-formation™". Why? Simple: that's what we've got!

One of the reasons we can make such a claim is that piloting really transforms people: not just how they are today, but what they once were. We know Freud said that the child is father of the man. We know that revisiting and making friends with our "inner child" is fantastical-ly powerful and healing. But we also somehow have to revisit that child and take away its hurts and griefs.

Otherwise we rise above our condition, only to drag it around with us for the rest of our existence. The child that was you was a special crea-ture; he or she must have been, to have given rise to such a wonderful creation as YOU. But the chances are that he or she hurt a great deal, was confused, upset and frightened, at least some of the time.

Lest this begin to sound like New Age psychobabble, let me assure you that it is precise and technical, exactly as set out below.

The Myth Of Time

We all sense time; or believe we do. Yet advanced physics is on the brink of declaring time nothing more than a convenient fiction. It's there to help equations and calculations but it probably doesn't exist.

There is a strong clue, which is—so far as physics is concerned—time could run just as well backwards as forwards. We can work backwards and figure out where an object WAS, providing we have the characteristics of its movement; we can work out where it WILL BE at some time in the future, same equations, same calculations.

Is this mere speculation or does it have any value?

The answer is a surprising, even shocking, YES! It's very helpful to dispose of time. What we are doing with piloting, in effect, is editing the time element. From having memonemes and charge stuck in the NOW, we re-process it and put it back in its proper place on the timeline. In doing so, the past loses is venom.

In fact one of the very simplest remedies you can run, when someone has been hurt, is to ask repetitively and alternately: *"Where did it happen?"* (time past) and *"Where are you now?"* (time present, new location). Sooner or later, inner knowing switches on the lights and says, "Hey, that was then, this is now!"

Try it! I dare you!

Thing is, we can use a friendly, malleable time factor to change our experience of the past. Since the past and our memories can impose trouble on our present-time being, then let's change the past and it's memories.

But, you say, that's cheating. That cannot work. The past is what it is; what happened was what happened and you can't change that.

Wrong!

It's another application of the 180-degree rule: the truth is the exact opposite of what everyone believes. It's a trick!

Why Do We Carry Around Hurtful Memories? ···········

There is no time past, since what WAS has gone, buried. Our only contact with what WAS is a set of memories we carry round. Why we choose to carry round the hurtful ones and, even more mysteriously, why we let them hurt us, is one of the great mysteries of consciousness and one I would like to solve before I drop this body.

Our past, then, is simply a facsimile copy of what happened to us, often imperfect. Our personal history in consciousness is only as meaningful and valid as we allow it to be. What I have discovered for myself is that it is possible to revisit these earlier memory experiences and alter them! I remind you of the words of Steve Ramirez at MIT (page 131): "We normally think of memory like a tape recorder or video of the past, but it's actually very reconstructive in nature." At the very least, we can change our perception of them, or perhaps both.

Gurus do this all the time! They make up fanciful stories that give them mystical powers and they start lording it over others. Do I believe that Moses was given tablets of stone, chiseled by God? Of course I don't. Nor that The Koran was immaculately conceived. Or that petty criminal Joseph Smith really found the Mormon tablets of gold (where are these enduring forms of writing? Why has no-one else seen them?)

The take home I'm offering is not that religions are fake: what people choose to believe is their own affair. All I am saying is that people can give themselves a colorful story and start to believe it. It works for them like a real history. They are empowered by this flim flam version of themselves (and maybe that turns out to be more important to them than whether or not other people believe the story or not).

L. Ron Hubbard, the founder of the Scientology movement, is a case in point. He built himself up with incredible stories about being a decorated war hero, a celebrated explorer, blind and crippled at the end of WW2 and yet clever enough to fully heal himself. It all turned out to be fake. Even his engineering doctorate was bought from a paper mill university for a few $100s.

It emerged, when his list of personal affirmations surfaced (written circa 1947), that he was an extremely insecure man, building himself up with what were part confessions, part wishes to be more powerful, more successful, and someone afraid of gonorrhea, sexual failure and seething with resentment toward Admiral Braystead.

So if it works for dudes on the make, why not use it as a valid technique? I'm not suggesting we encourage people to lie about their resume or who they really are. But it is possible to share with a pilot a different version of one's past that makes more sense and creates delight instead of shame, courage instead of fear. Why ever not?

I've tested it repeatedly and it works wonderfully well.

GSR Signs

It's worth pointing out that the GSR meter responds exactly the same to re-engineered history as it does to original memories! That's because the subconscious mind has no real way of telling the difference. Remember "identity thinking" (X=Y=Z), page 81? That's the basic physiological mode or lizard sense.

Everything equals everything else.

Thus the GSR meter, which is supposedly a lie detector (but isn't) responds just as it would to a real memory.

That's telling us something powerful: like it or not; makes sense or not; *made up memories work just as well as real ones.* So if you were some cowardly solder on the battlefield, who ran away at the first sight of weapons, you will feel cold and creepy when you revive the memory. But if you substitute that for a different scenario, in which you unsheathed your sword, rushed straight at the enemy and led the winning charge, wouldn't you feel warm, proud and excited... thrilled even?

That's different physiology at work.

Let me just point out that the physiology is what counts. That's the determinant of how you feel about yourself. Why not wear the new coat of many colors, if it fits?

The thing is, we can even run "future memories", which are not yet real. But they process just the same. If someone is sure to die and a family member will be extremely distraught, run the "death" as if it was already happening. It will get them in a far calmer place for when the real moment finally arrives.

Just as we can speculate over choice futures (two or more alternatives), we can similarly process two different pasts. "Alternative histories" have big power, trust me!

You cannot say this is the same as telling a lie, for goodness' sake. This is editing or tweaking the time element of "memory", is all. We still get shift and still get occasional peak experiences. *How punk is that?*

A Bit More Theory and Background

There's a famous demo that on-stage gurus sometimes pull: they yell, "Snake!" and fling a crawly wiggly "creature" into the audience. When the panic and screams die down, smarty pants explains how it's just a rubber imitation snake.

Everyone relaxes; the guru goes on to explain the mind responded just as if it was really a snake. What does that tell you? The subconscious mind, which generates all the fear, doesn't know the truth. It just does what it does.

And surprisingly, that's the same for memory... [don't do this!]: if you were to create pictures in your mind of being stripped, beaten and robbed, you'd feel pretty grim, pretty soon; you know you would.

It's a fake memoneme (unpleasant experience), but it plays on you just like the real thing. Therefore good memories, even if made up to suit, do the opposite and make you feel good. What's wrong with that?

Alfred Korzybski made famous the phrase "the map is not the territory"; specifically, he meant our mental map is not the experience, only a copy of it.

We could rewrite the card file of memory and make it say something we would rather was written there. In other words, we can change the map. We haven't altered the real life experience, or objective history one jot. But we have sure adjusted our personal history because it now only exists in those records. Put more philosophically, we haven't altered reality, only the memory of that reality.

In Korzybski's metaphor, we have altered the map but not the terrain. Since it is the map which tells us how we feel, the results of doing this can have far-reaching results for the individual.

We get a second chance, in effect.

Remember, the client is aware there has been a deliberate change. It is not as if we are trying to hoodwink him or her and slip something past the soul or consciousness! Since it isn't introduced below the level of awareness (ie. hypnotically), it does not pose a threat to articulate rationalization.

Yet it works. Altering memory can be just like living life all over again. In fact here we have the core problem with entities (see page 198, The Complex Of Self): each of these brings a different history and thus a different conscious awareness. The confusion comes from having different histories in the same thought process, not *de facto* from altered accounts of the objective past.

More Science To Back Me Up

The other day I was reading a fascinating paper about work done at The Institute for Consciousness and Dream Research in Vienna, Austria. I instantly recognized it as a version of this process I developed back in the 1990s. They were using lucid dreaming therapeutically. Lucid dreams, you may know, are those where we are in a sense conscious and can control what happens in the dream. Researchers have shown that by having the patient dream up different outcomes—those with a happy ending—they were to a considerable degree healed of their nightmares, PTSD trauma, or whatever.

According to Brigitte Holzinger, lead researcher at the Institute, one patient even figured out how, within a nightmare, to go back to the point before the threat emerged and continue the dream in a different direction!

The results have been very successful (Oh, yes, Brigitte, I could have told you that 2 decades ago!) It is now speculated that manipulating dreams in this way could help with our creativity.

Many people find inspiration in sleep. Dmitri Mendeleev famously dreamed up the structure of the periodic table of elements, one of sciences most brilliant tools. The melody for that most beautiful of all Beatles tunes *Yesterday* came to Paul McCartney while he was dreaming.

[*New Scientist*, 18 Feb 2017, vol. 233 No 3113, pp. 32-35]

Bending History

There are two basic techniques to change historical reality in piloting. The first is to re-run what actually did happen, but to change the resulting feelings or appreciation of what was present in that experience. Maybe it needs tweaking a little. This way we unload the charge caused by the disparity between what did happen and what the individual felt ought to have happened.

The second approach is to run an *entirely new experience* in the place of the old one. The client was in a messy divorce situation; tempers constantly flared and he or she said terrible things to their spouse. Maybe there was physical violence... chairs flying, crocks smashed, silly actions that no-one should have engaged in.

Years later, he or she regrets the nasty and abusive behavior and wants to make amends. Well, we allow that. We can transport the person in a fantasy dream of having done far better; behaved more rationally; spoken kinder and soothing words. This not only feels different, it changes events. There is a new library card file.

Not surprisingly, this can have an individual feeling more courageous and appreciated in this lifetime. It will certainly clear the distress of the earlier failure.

In fact both techniques can do this for us.

The only thing I have observed is we can't amputate history too drastically! Someone who went through WW2 and was hurt by it might run feeling good at most stress points, instead feeling bad. But you couldn't run the history that Hitler was never born, there was no WW2, and he or she stayed home, happily, on the farm.

When To Do This

You can do it right after a bad experience—running heavy traumas. It's a good way to lift emotions. You will (hopefully) have cleared the charge. But it can still leave the client a trifle dazed and even chagrined.

If you have other viewpoints to deal with, or you have used one of the remedies in chapter 13, then you can probably continue.

But once in a while, it is good practice to break out of running the negative and deliberately choose to process the positive.

You can certainly do it on someone who has come from another practice or technique and needs a lift. Take up the same experiences the other practitioner did and enhance them with some fun and excitement.

Tell the client what you are going to do. You may need to fully explain, if he or she is uncomfortable with "fake memories". Better explain this isn't really running a lie. It is running an important truth, which is that: *things could have been better!*

You might encounter a little protest. Obviously, there will be computations such as "If I had done it that way instead of what happened, I would never have lost my job and so I would now be doing..." But we don't want to start creating alternative universes. Just coax them through what DID happen, with the new feeling, rather than some totally alien reality, unless that is important to the client. In which case, let them get on with it.

Ask the client "Tell me how that experience [we just addressed] could be improved for you" or "Is there a better version of events you would find empowering instead of painful?" He or she will want to be resourceful and at cause, naturally.

Once the client is experienced, you can ask them "How should it have been?" or "Put yourself at cause".

Run this new version of events, exactly like before.

Make this memory come to life, really live it.

Move to the beginning... Tell me what's happening.

Now, talk me though it, just as if it's really happening.

If you are using a GSR meter, watch the meter fly. It's as if you are running the charge all over again (which in fact you are doing!) Continue until the meter shows no further reaction and there is a new awareness, especially a different thought, feeling, attitude or whatever.

When it is thoroughly flattened, and if you have been drilled on what to do, you can re-order later events, by scanning up to the now, seeing each related episode—albeit briefly—given a new lick of paint and a new outcome too!

Re-Ordering The Timeline

It won't just affect the incidents on the chain, but ALL life's experiences after the new version of events.

For the more experienced individual, you can simply direct them by instructing "Re-work the timeline up to the present, changing things with this new empowering experience".

For someone who is new, ask them to move forward along the timeline—quickly but not skipping—to the present, seeing each event transformed by the "new history" you just planted.

If he or she is now full of self-confidence and dynamism, it stands to reason that he or she will get the girl or boy they dreamed of. There will be no rejections when dating, no failures at college, they will pass the auditions to go to acting school and they will be short-listed and get any job they choose.

I've seen people with little or no sales experience go out and close significant deals within hours of this procedure. One guy picked up a book, started studying that same day, and eventually went to college.

Suddenly, the life they could have lived—the life the wanted to live—is available to them as an empowering "memory". It's a marvelous life hack. A new map gives a new psychic terrain. Korzybski's truth is very powerful indeed.

You can even take a small aspect of some unpleasant events and tweak it. Ask the client to change a small portion of it and then run it that way. Meaning this:

"Get the picture to yourself doing that or saying that... back then."

Do not let him or her think of doing it someday in the future. You are attempting to alter the past with this!

Punk Points:

- "Truth is relative", I've heard it said. That may or may not be so. But truth, the real truth, is a highly subjective thing. Being forced to agree with what other people claim is fact is not very empowering. Telling your own story the way you want it told is actually therapeutic.

- Wasn't it Joseph Campbell who told us that we need myths to live by? Well, we can do long-range myths, like gods and goddesses. But closer to home we find our own personal myths. These are precious and self-serving, self-enlightening even. What's wrong with that?

- The mystery of memory is why we hug the hurtful ones close to us and treat the glorious ones with disdain. Isn't that kind of crazy? Maybe we should all learn a better way. Re-writing personal history is just one better way!

- It worked for Jesus, Mohammed and Buddha! At one time they were just kids. But somewhere along the line, each one gave himself a new "history": the Son of God, the Great Prophet, the Awakened One, or whatever.

- Don't be fooled by time. It's not an absolute at all.

CHAPTER 20

THE PROTOPLASM ENTITY (PE)

Protoplasm is the living being on the lowest level. [*The Origin Nature and Evolution of Protoplasmic Individuals and Their Associations*, By Faustino Cordon, Pergamon Press, Oxford and New York, 1982, p. 133]

In opening out the timeline with a bandsaw, as we do with Hypnoetics™ and Supernoetics® piloting, we of course encounter numerous past lives. Regardless of whether you believe in reincarnation or not, these memories arise. But we encounter an added dimension to this complexity. There is a biological "being" or entity, derived from the protoplasm line. We call this the *Protoplasm Entity (PE)*. It also has memory and it has a real case. The PE also has "past lives", or a timeline of its own. These protoplasm memories also influences the Complex Of Self, specifically what I have referred to here as the "creature" self.

I'm going beyond just body memory now, into fascinating new realms, only lately explored by me. Any half decent memory worker/therapist/counselor (yes, there are some!) knows that stress and trauma are visited on the body. Any unresolved misery or psychic trauma can result in physical symptoms: aches and pains; actual disease processes; masses; sensations; strange subjective feelings and even deformity.

I'm now talking IMPACT: actual force impinged in the body, but not from violence—from psychic injury.

This genetic being is not entirely physical. Or more exactly, let me say that it is an information field imprint. It manifests in the physical.

Homeopaths would be familiar with this principle, as so-called miasms; a sort of shadow or imprint on the genetic line. It's not in the genes or even the epigenes. It's not even physical (see below).

You might wonder how it is transferred from organism to organism, generation to generation. Even if it was a physical imprint, it would have to pass through the zygote—the initial fusion of the male and female halves or "gametes", which come together at conception.

That's the equivalent to a one-cell organism and, remarkable though it seems, people have been able to recall that moment—the "conception dream", as it's called—so memory is operating in some form or other, even at this very early moment.

We don't know how this memory transfer takes place is the honest answer. Non-physical doesn't mean it isn't there and doesn't happen. It just means there is no "stuff" or matter version of the memory.

In fact that doesn't entirely rule out a physical transfer. Consider the holograph model. Most people think of the 3-D property of a hologram. But the really important characteristic of a hologram is that if you divide it in half, you don't end up with two half picture. You end up with two smaller entire (whole) pictures.

If you cut these smaller pictures in half, you end up with four complete pictures; then eight; then sixteen and so on, to infinity.

Of course these smaller and smaller images get fainter and fainter but each is nonetheless complete. So—the reasoning goes—the code for the entire cosmos is present in your fingernail or a pimple at the end of your nose!

Holographic memory then would be a small trace that holds all the information in question. If the universe is truly a hologram (which is widely accepted, through far from proven), then ancestral memories could pass through the tiny zygote single-cell phase complete and entire.

The Theta Line vs. The Protoplasm Line ··················

Let's clarify the differences here. Basically, the theta being is free to come and go whenever and wherever it wishes. We encounter beings with past lives in different times and places, as different genders, sometimes as animals or objects (not just living creatures), and from countless other worlds, dimensions and universes. Basically, a theta being can consider itself to be anywhere in creation and thus that's where it is.

The protoplasm line, however, isn't so free. Each protoplasm entity must come from a prior protoplasm entity: the progenitor. By definition it will inhabit the same or similar places, not far apart geographically and immediately sequential in time.

The theta being could be an earthly monk in one lifetime, a Babylonian whore the next, and captain of a silver spaceship somewhere in the Arcturus system after that. Let your imagination run wild.

Whereas the protoplasm line will be (say) Italian aristocracy for several generations, maybe with a painter thrown in; then Italian peasantry, after that, for several more generations; a count of Austrian descent, after the invasion of Lombardy; the daughter of a Milan industrialist and now a university undergraduate in Rome. Get the idea?

Viking Memory

I like sharing the following example: for many years (decades) I had a completely stuck picture of a wild scene in northern Europe, around the tenth century. The whole scene had a very Viking feel.

I was sitting on a clifftop, holding upright a massive sword, waiting; the Sun was setting to the west in a rage of blood-red light. Clearly, there was going to be an encounter and it was not going to be good!

I tried every way to date this picture, get some truth, that would make it vanish. It stuck fast.

Then—Duh!—one day I remembered my Viking ancestry. The name Mumby is a Norse name. A whole longboat full of Mumbys rowed across from Denmark to what is now England in the 10th century, landed on a small strip of beach and founded a village which, to this day, is called Mumby (7 miles north of the coastal town of Skegness). Over a thousand years later, all my father's family came from within fifty miles of this village.

Of course, I get it! This memory was not "mine", which is why I could get rid of it (wrong ownership). It belonged to the Protoplasm Entity. I was able to reason that whatever this "encounter" was, my ancestor must have been the winner, and gone on to spread his seed, otherwise I would not have been here!

Anyway, spotting the truth caused this wild image to become evanescent and I have not been able to recall it since, except as a memory of a memory.

The Heart's Code

You may have heard of extraordinary cases in which organ transplant cases have taken on memories from the donor. That's memories from the PE, of course.

One of the most memorable was an American woman named Claire Sylvia, who received a new heart at a hospital in Yale, Connecticut. She was told that her donor was an eighteen year-old male from Maine, USA who had just died in a motorcycle accident.

Soon after the operation, Sylvia declared that she felt like drinking beer, something she hadn't particularly been fond of. Later, she observed an uncontrollable urge to eat chicken nuggets and found herself drawn to visiting the popular chicken restaurant chain, KFC. She also began craving green peppers which she hadn't particularly liked before.

It emerged in due course that the heart donor used to love chicken nuggets, green peppers and beer. [Sylvia, Claire. A Change of Heart: a memoir. New York; Warner Books, 1997].

The celebrated book The Heart's Code by Paul Pearsall MD, describes the stories of seventy-three heart transplant patients, and sixty-seven other organ transplant recipients.

One of the most striking examples, was that of an eight year-old girl, who received the heart of a murdered ten year-old girl, and began having recurring vivid nightmares about the murder. Her mother arranged a consultation with a psychiatrist who after several sessions concluded that she was witnessing the actual physical incidents in her mind's eye. They decided to call the police who used the detailed descriptions of the murder given by the eight year-old (the time, the weapon, the place, the clothes he wore, what the little girl he killed had said to him) to find and convict the man in question.

This was a complete and verified PE memory. It could have been run and cleared using Hypnoetics™!

[Pearsall, Paul. *The Heart's code: tapping the wisdom and power of our heart energy*. New York; Broadway Books, 1999].

Under the jokey title "Art Transplant", the British tabloid newspaper, *The Daily Mail*, ran a story in 2006 about William Sheridan, a retired catering manager with poor drawing skills, who suddenly developed artistic talents after a heart transplant operation. It was later discovered that the heart donor had been a keen and competent artist.

["The Art Transplant" The Daily Mail March 31,2006. http://www.dailymail.co.uk/health/article-381589/The-art-transplant.html]

If you have the opportunity to help in such a case, simply engage with the organ part by talking to it directly. Ask its story and process it, just like any other memory episode. It will be very like a past life memory. Expect a dialogue and you will get it. If there is any interference from the case in front of you, ask him or her if they would mind stepping aside while you talk to the part. He or she will need to relay your instructions to the organ telepathically, as it were.

If you are able to work on a case in this way, you will have made a start in understanding the multi-part nature of "self" described in chapter 17 as "The Complex Of Self."

Ancestral Curses ··

You may be familiar with the concept that certain families seem to be some sort of a 'jinx' (for the want of a better word) of accidents, disasters, setbacks and untimely and sudden deaths, sometimes stretching back a few hundred years.

These are basically protoplasm shadows or imprints, playing out. In other words, genetic memories. These are very real and you will encounter them frequently, once you know to be alert for them.

There may be a legend or tradition that Wild Minnie of the Clan Fergus laid a curse on great great great Uncle Rory! It runs down through the generations.

We take the implanting of the curse as a legitimate episode, get the time and place

and process it (it would run like a past life, of course).

Many tribes and races take curses very seriously. Voodoo is big business in the Caribbean, for example. There are many reported instances, which check out authentically, where a malevolent person has cast a curse on someone and it comes to pass. What is not so easy to disentangle is whether or not it is subconsciously made to come true by the person who is the target and believes in the power of the curse; or whether there is the possibility of real psychic force that overrides an individual's auto-determinism.

Really, too much is made of curses, taboos, and malevolent beings, ghosts, wicked monsters, voodoo, devils and the like. They have NO POWER whatever over a person, except the power that is invested in them by the person who chooses to believe these things can affect him or her.

If you are afraid and believe such a thing could hurt you... guess what? You can be hurt! But if you utterly reject such a possibility (you should) then another's intentions cannot harm you.

Bottom line? A curse does not take its power from the wisher or giver; a curse takes ALL its power from the target or victim.

Parental Dysfunctionality

Don't get this idea of charge and aberration passed down through the generations mixed up with parental stupidity and ignorance...

The sad fact is that parents pass their crap down to their children, who pass it to their children, etc. Whatever issues the parents have, the child is in danger of acquiring the same, sometimes even before the child can think properly and independently.

I can reveal something even more interesting; it needs further research and development. But about 10 years ago Vivien and I were investigating the effects of voice re-patterning, along the lines of Alfred Tomatis' work. We used a device called the Vo-Cal 360, developed by inventor Calvin Young.

What we found repeatedly was that it was not so much the parents that "imprinted" on the child, as Freud claimed. It was the grandparents.

Grandfather is a big deal in North American Indian lore; Chinese tradition too. After this insight, I am inclined to believe these old and venerable wisdoms more than Freud!

Of course parents are important. But in later piloting, we have developed the technique of interviewing the client about his or her grandparents. And you know what's amazing? The person doesn't even need to have met the grandparent. Maybe he or she died long before the child was even born. But you can ask: "What do you know about your father's father?" and so on, through all four figures. You will get interesting answers and the GSR meter will respond.

You will find events from the past and, yes, you will know and see enough in your mind's eye to process these as your own memories. We call this trans-personal memory and Stanislav Grof researched it thoroughly and wrote a book you may enjoy: *Beyond The Brain* (1985).

Yes, parents are often bad news. But where did they get their "stuff" from? Their parents, of course, and so on, back through the generations.

I have yet to ascertain for certain this is the way to go in order to disconnect everyone from their ancestral garbage via the PE (hopefully without disconnecting them from ancestral wisdom). But if I am right, we have a way at last of stopping the passing on of stupidity, wild emotions, dysfunctional behaviors and all the other human curses! Many workers have tried to solve this problem. SOMEBODY has to solve it, otherwise civilization is going nowhere.

Miasms

A miasm is one of the most powerful influences in health and disease I know, yet the least acknowledged or understood. The word was introduced by Samuel Hahnemann, the father of homeopathy, but I prefer to think of a 'genetic toxin', since that gives a far clearer idea of what we think we are dealing with. Basically a miasm means a shadow or disease 'imprint' which is inherited down the generations.

All acutely observant doctors are aware that disease and disturbance tends to run in families. It can be likened to a kind of family blight. This is not to mean a specific replicated genetic disorder carried by the genes like, for example, haemophilia or Freidrich's ataxia. The sickliness can manifest itself in various ways, each individual suffering differently from the others in his or her family tree but all bound by the commonality of being a somewhat weakened or unhealthy bunch, because of the miasm.

This idea may seem to be an attempt to revive Lamarck's discredited theory of evolution, which said that an organism's responses to environmental stressors could be passed on to offspring. This is now held not to be true; the Darwinian/Mendelian dogma reigns, that only the factors carried in the genes can be inherited. But that's wrong, basically!

To Hahnemann a miasm was something more in the nature of a primitive illness, a throwback. He named three in particular: *Syphilis, Sycosis* and *Psora*. Briefly, syphilis (or *Luesinum*) has ulcerating tendencies; sycosis or *Medorrhinum* (meaning from gonorrhoea) is congestive, leading to deposits and tumor formation; while psora (*Psorinum*) is a protean disturbance that relates to functional imbalances of all kinds.

Antoine Nebel and Henry C Allen added *Tuberculinum*, which many practitioners now regard as the pre-eminent miasm; indeed it is still troubling us today and TB has begun a comeback, despite antibiotics. Among the fall-out diseases from this inherited toxin one can list asthma, eczema, hay fever, food allergies, chronic sinusitis, migraines, mental illness of various kinds, irritable bowel, colitis, heart trouble, diabetes, Hodgkin's disease and even leukemia.

Leon Vannier added a fifth, which is the *oncotic* (cancer) miasm. It is characterized by changes in body odour, warts, excrescences, sores that refuse to heal and a sallow skin, somewhat like that of malignant cachexia.

All this will rightly cause you to think of the possibility of unhappy psychological states also being caused by miasms. You would not be wrong.

Be on the alert for miasms adding difficulties to the person's psychological case, especially the protoplasm entity. See, even though miasms are energetic or even non-material, it is the physical body that is disturbed; the creature.

It would be heading in the wrong direction to blame the theta being.

As an example of how miasmata (the plural) indirectly impinge on our work, consider a person who is angry and bites, which suggests the Syphilinum (Luesinum) miasm. He is orally fixated according to Freud's theory.

Samuel Hahnemann described *psora* as characterized by the feeling that we are small, weak, unable to succeed in the face of a challenge, overwhelmed by the demands that life makes on us. It is the feeling of lack—lack of strength, stamina, power, or whatever else it takes to survive. *Psora* is the influence that makes us feel we can never have enough money, comfort, belongings, or love.

It can help to administer the miasm, before wasting scores of piloting hours addressing those very issues!

Biological Function of The PE

In the end, the genetic or Protoplasm Entity has a job to do. It's there as a compilation of ancestral memories, to guide, help and protect you. We are not in the job of trying to override Nature's positive mechanisms.

What we are seeking to do it spread the light of truth, so there are no dark unknowns. And in doing so, we disconnect the vicious override mechanisms by which remote and now-worthless reactive or reductionist memories are forced into the current thinking train, where they have no positive value but are counter-productive.

Instinct is one thing. But conditioned reflexes, enforced by experiences that took place long ago and now have no relevance, are the very curse of human nature!

Wilhelm Reich, who orthodox medicine is pleased to describe as "discredited", had one abiding idea (no, not orgone). It was the Emotional Plague. In Reich's view this was the number one disease which threatened Mankind.

Look around you—and at past history—and take a note of the outcomes of all fear, rages, hatred and intolerance. The Emotional Plague has killed hundreds of millions, through acts of violence, destruction and war. Throw in famine (through selfishness and stupidity) and economic deprivation (through greed and stupidity), environmental damage (through ignorance and stupidity) and you will readily admit that Mankind's emotional ineptness and passion for irrationality has, indeed, cost many billions of lives.

There's a lot to write about on this topic. For the meantime, just fully flatten whatever you find, whether it is psychic memory or residues in the PE.

Punk Points:

- However "spiritual" you want to be and however clever you rate yourself at psychic abilities, it's all for nothing if you neglect the body. Rejecting the flesh is very foolish and ignorant. The truth is, that the physical is as much "you" as the theta being.

- As we progress up the ladder with Supernoetics® renewal, we emerge more and more as a powerful spiritual entity. We are gloriously magnificent in this state. Wonder and awe are too slight-ish words to even begin to express it.

- Yet we are also "creature". It's the lowest level of thinking. But it's still real. The "creature", or what I here call the Protoplasm Entity (PE), is still going to serve up unpleasant emotions, daft behaviors, appetites and obsessions of all kinds (sexual, not the least of these). Unless you work with and alongside your "creature" and cherish it you'll be very uncomfortable indeed.

- Think of the PE like a thoroughbred animal. You would stroke it, love it and care for it. Feed it well; get it the best veterinary care; exercize it; put it out to stud maybe! Thoroughbreds are enormously valuable. Don't mistreat yours.

- Learn to step back or, as we say, go "upstairs" and see yourself being yourself when emotions get too strong. From on high you can calm, soothe and even advize the creature. You are NOT your emotions. You are NOT your behaviors. You are not even your thoughts. You are the point of knowing and awareness at the heart of everything that matters.

CHAPTER 21

BETTER COMMUNICATION MEANS FASTER RESULTS

Supernoetics® (the parent philosophy of Hypnoetics™) has a lot to offer in the field of improved communication. Pilots—even amateur pilots— need to have above average communication skills.

It's important to be able to stay on track, not be distracted by displays of emotion and not to let the person dodge the issues by mindless chatter or distractions. Yet this is a common social gaff.

You can start off on one topic and, within minutes, find yourselves over

the hill and far away, talking about something completely new (off-topic)!

Here are some simple techniques to guide you in what works best and to create what we call "communication boxing", which is to say holding a safe "box" in which to contain communication with the client. This boxing idea works pretty well in life too! Practice it and then try it.

In many ways, good communication skills are the key to almost any success and any pleasure in life. It's that important!

Let's start with the anatomy of communications.

Strokes

A stroke is start-to-finish of a communication sequence. It's basically impulse, response and closer.

The impulse can be a question, a comment, a touch, a look even. A bullet is a communication stroke but don't look for a lively reply!

Basically, successful communication is when you get the intended outcome. But it is important to note that, in Supernoetics®, we do not lay all the responsibility on the receiver. Whatever the source-point or origin of the communication intended to convey, *the actual meaning of a communication is the effect it has.*

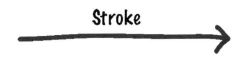

We do not accept the excuse: I didn't mean that... In a later section we'll look at loops within loops and the important preliminary loop asks: Is the person ready to receive the communication? If he or she is not in the right frame of mind to receive your communication as intended, don't say it!

We can represent the basic stroke diagrammatically as follows:

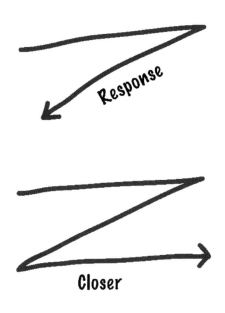

The Response

By response we mean something that is appropriate and relevant. *What time is it? Go to Hell*, is not an appropriate response to the question and should not be validated with a closer.

You don't have to agree with the person's answer or response, provided that it is appropriate. People may say things that startle or shock you. But the key question is whether or not it is a suitable response.

What party did you vote for? May attract the answer: *Them bastards? I don't give no politicians a single second of thought. All aughta be drowned!* It's entirely appropriate, even if not quite the tone or answer you were looking for!

The Closer

Don't be puzzled about that term. It just means whatever ends off the stroke. We sometimes call this an acknowledgement. It's the "full stop" or end-signal. But it needn't be any sophisticated phrase. Just a smile will do sometimes.

Remember every process loop has a beginning, a process and an end. This is just the end-marker. It closes the loop.

The closer is often omitted but is important. It lets the other person know that their response was received and is duly acknowledged.

So:

- *What do you want to do today?*
- *Let's go to the zoo.*
- *Awesome!*

Non-verbal:

- A smile
- A return smile
- A nod of thanks or thumbs up; shows the reply smile has been noted and enjoyed!

Distractions

Sometimes the person wants to lead off in some other direction or won't answer the question, directly or indirectly. Well then, we have to bring it back under control. We politely but firmly re-iterate our question or topic.

Here's an example:

- *I am returning this faulty clock. Can I please have my money back?*

- *Come back another day, please Madam.*

- *That will not be necessary as I am here now. Please return my payment as the clock is faulty.*

- *I'll check the product then Madam.*

- *Thank you.*

Irrelevancies

Stroke

Distraction

Repeat
Re-affirm

Response

Closer

People can be very bad at this. Here's an outrageous example, with lots of distractions:

- *When is Uncle Jed's birthday?*

- *I don't know, I can never keep track of dates.*

- *Well, get yourself one of those smartphones, which has calendars and things.*

- *What, you think I'm crazy?*

- *iPhones are pretty good. What's your problem?*

- *That jerk Steve Jobs, he didn't treat people right.*
- *Lots of business big shots don't. Why are you picking on him?*
- *What, are you some kinda commie?*

This is opening loop after loop and closing none. It's inefficient. It's also slightly psychotic! Sooner or later, it will to a breakdown in communication—usually very quickly.

Then there is the rarer person, who speaks in endless nesting (one inside the other) sentences, like this:

Einstein was a bit of a... Mind you, most men are... Not like the fairer sex... Women seem to have a sort of different... In fact my mother was the worst at this... Really...

You've probably met someone like this and found them baffling and tiring. You cannot easily follow the speaker's thread of thought. Why tiring? Because endless incomplete loops cause fatigue. Their problem is they can't close loops.

To be efficient, we want our stroke out, an immediate and acceptable response and a closer out, to make it clear we are satisfied thus far...

Concerns

However, it may sometimes happen that a person has a genuine concern, which he or she wants dealt with, before giving you a suitable response. If the concern is real and genuine, you are bound to handle it and not go blustering on. Put the person's mind at rest and then chase your desired response.

Concerns could be almost anything. Something is worrying them, they see something hidden in the question, a discomfort, they are not quite sure what you are after (but will respond nicely, once they are on your side), there is a time issue... and so on.

There are as many concerns as there are people to talk to at any given moment. The criterion you use is that *they are concerned*, not just trying to deflect you.

- *Do you use Gorgadent toothpaste?*
- *Who wants to know?*
- *It's just a survey I'm doing.*
- *You won't use my name?*
- *No, not at all.*
- *Can't stand the stuff, it tastes disgusting!*

Visually, here's what this one looks like:

Concerns

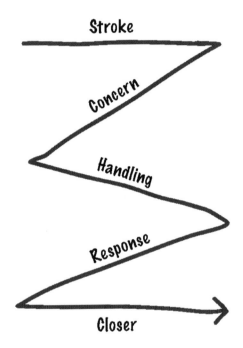

For pilots, this skill is crucial.

- *Remember a time you were stood up on a date.*
- *I can't, I'll just burst into tears.*
- *Don't worry about that. We'll clear all the emotional charge from it.*
- *But that's embarrassing.*
- *Sincerely, you do need to share with me, otherwise I can't help.*

- *I remember one time, a nice guy, I really liked him... (bursts into tears).*

But you see she has begun responding properly, once she was put at ease.

Commands ···

Sometimes we don't want a verbal response, we want the other person to follow instructions. We can drill this too:

- *Pass me that book*
- (The person does so)
- *Thank you.*

Then the coach or mentor starts to get tricky and won't obey the command. He or she may throw up distractions, which are dealt with as above. Then we practice handling genuine concerns, before insisting on our command.

When drilling this, we don't allow disobedience. We politely push and push and push. Then—once we get the response we wanted—we use a nice friendly closer: Great! Note that *force majeure* is NOT part of this learning.

Our pilots have to become naturals at this. Occasionally a person becomes dopey or upset in a flight and you want to maintain control, to get him or her through.

Closing the loop is important discipline in the question of controlling a person or group in life. It's therapeutic for the student to drill this firmness and insistence. It also does a bit of good for the peer mentor who is coaching too! Fact. Respect for closing loops is therapeutic for everyone.

Notice that screaming and yelling are no part of getting a response from someone disobedient. We want *firmness*, not the usual emotional hysterics. This is one of the places where practiced and controlled communication skills really come into their own. Anything other than firm and polite business-like speech is counter-productive and is what commonly lowers the tone of proceedings or even leads to a quarrel (a crash of accord).

Extreme Resistance or Willful Non-Cooperation ········

We have an answer to non-cooperation and disobedience. We make it happen and then still say: *Thank you!* Just as if the person had done what was asked willingly.

Verbal persuasion may tax your diplomatic skills to the limit! Still, being able to negotiate against willful resistance is a considerable life skill, well worth acquiring!

Taken to the full, we physically enforce the command, taking the person's hand or hands, placing them on the book, and then sliding it towards our own position. When done, we still use the close: *Well done!*

In fact you can do this with unconscious people.

- *Give me your hand*
- (take it anyway and then give the closer)
- *Thank you.*

Do this repeatedly and don't be surprised if, sooner or later, he or she gives you the hand. "Unconscious" people are not so out of it as doctors and scientists like to think.

Children ···

The previous hack can be applied to kids out of control with considerable effect. If the child is having a tantrum, writhing around and screaming, invite him or her to take control of themselves by applying the command process.

It's very simple. Just say: "Touch that doorknob," make him or her do it, by gently taking their hand and touching the doorknob, then giving the closer. You use a calm tone of voice, like this is just a kind of fun game, not an enforcement.

You can choose a doorknob, a table, chair, the wall, anything that comes to mind, providing it is within the child's reach. Move around the room.

Smile as you go and give rewarding closers, as if you are pleased with the response. Never threaten or get heavy in this hack. NEVER.

You will find that in less than a minute a wildly out of control child can be calmed and brought to reason. He or she will be touching objects just by being prompted, no force required.

That's if you make it rewarding.

Clarification

Sometimes the person needs a detail clarified, before he or she will answer to their own satisfaction. This step simply follows the pattern above:

- *Tell me something about books*

- *Do you want me to include thoughts about digital books?*

- *Sure. Those too.*

- *OK, well I think books are just about the coolest human invention of all time.*

- *Thanks.*

Here's the schematic:

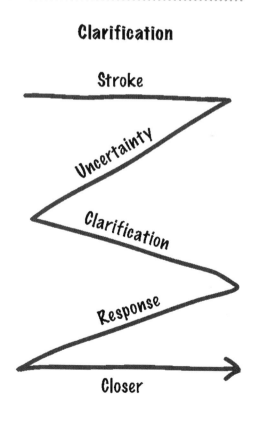

There can be mixes, of course. Clarification plus concern might look like this:

- *Can you remember anything about your time at college?*
- *I'm tired. Can we sit down while we talk?*
- *Sure.*
- They sit down and the conversation gets under way...

Exercises

These strokes and loops repay careful rehearsal. These are important life skills. Exercises are simple to do and competence in the face of all issues and provocation is *required* for piloting and tutor training.

The student and peer mentor sit opposite each other. If the preliminary exercises, Holding Your Space and Improving Voice Delivery are weak, these need to be drilled first.

Otherwise the coach mentor sets up a variety of responses and the student peer has to deal with them appropriately.

The coach mentor starts by reading aloud the name of each situation, followed by the handling. The student peer has to be able to describe each method of dealing with the situation, after being prompted.

So:

Peer mentor tests student: *Concerns-stroke-uncertainty-clarification-response-closer.* Now you... concerns?

Student: *Concerns-stroke-uncertainty-clarification-response-closer.*

Coach: *Good!*

When the student can rattle off the sequences, in any order, rapidly and correctly, mentor then proceeds to invent likely replies and responses. The student must deal with them, according to this section.

The student can graduate when he or she is smooth, unrufflable and relaxed at dealing with any and all curves thrown by the mentor.

Open and Closed Questions ·····································

There are two important types of question:

The closed question, which demands a single answer. For example: "How old are you?" "What time is it?" "Did you go to the concert last night?"

The open question, which projects no set limit of information. For example, ask for further clarification of a closed question: "What was the concert like?"

We can practice this distinction. With your peer mentor, ask a closed question followed by an open question.

The mentor coach partner gives the answers to each of these questions. To show you have listened properly, repeat or paraphrase the answer to the open question back to your coach, who corrects you or gives the closer if you duplicated their answer properly.

When receiving an answer to your open question, sometimes it helps to show you are listening and understanding by giving a half closer—this is not a strong full stop that would close the communication loop prematurely, but just a small nod of the head or "hm-hm" "uh-hu" or similar, that helps to keep the flow going.

When you have this mastered, then swap over roles.

Non-Reactive ··

Also, the requirement not to be emotionally reactive in response to the other does not mean you should be impassive. For example, you would respond naturally to a humorous remark by smiling, or even laughing, or say, "I understand" or "Wow. Thank you for sharing that. I'm honored" to an intimate secret.

However, two things it is very important NOT TO DO:

1. Correct, contradict or negate the information that you obtain.

2. Impose your point of view about the information received.

In piloting, these are the BIG SINS, as the aim of piloting is to encourage the individual to express their feelings, to look newly and without fear, in order to see more clearly. The person needs to discover truths for themselves, and any contradiction or imposed point of view ruins the process.

Even in everyday relationships, to invalidate the other's opinion or to give your irrelevant or premature evaluation is most unhelpful. Give facts and ask pertinent questions, but never tell someone they are wrong or give your opinion before they ask you.

[see also *A Gentleperson's Guide To Good Behavior*. 24 Apr 2014 Issue #: AE-240414]

Punk Points:

- Communication falls naturally into loops that we call "strokes". An origination (such as a question or command) is followed by a response, is followed by a closer (an acknowledgement). The closer completes the stroke.

- It is important, for efficiency, to keep control of strokes and not let them fall apart by virtue of drifting off with extra thoughts and distractions. This is what usually happens in every day speech: listen objectively! Pilots are drilled until they naturally maintain the discipline of strokes, while not becoming stilted or robotic.

- The client has the right to express concerns or request clarifications. We deal with these respectfully. Mere avoidance we correct gently and bring the current stroke back to its intended outcome.

- There is a larger communication loop that should not be lost sight of: the client is saying, "I need help," or "This could be good!" You respond, "Sure. We can work together and get some improved outcomes."

- Curiosity and interest are versions of concerns and clarifications. These are welcome.

CHAPTER 22

THE UNDERCUT

This, in a sense, is the super-punk part of the story. It could be argued this should be chapter 1 but I wanted to save it till last, to get you comfortably settled in to what we do!

We may be missing an important trick here; something to do even before piloting. We need to educate the piloting client (PC) on certain "facts of life". Specifically, where emotions come from.

Most people have no clue about emotions. They use language like "He makes me mad," and "You upset me," to other people. Of course the truth is *we do emotions to ourselves*. There are toxic people, it is true. But they can't lay emotions on you! You lay them on yourself!

Pretending other people cause your feelings is to surrender your power! If everyone grasped this one fact, the world would be transformed overnight.

The Muslims would have to learn, for instance, that Christians do not upset Muslims by being "disrespectful" to their teachings. Christians may not speak fondly of Islam—but getting upset about it is something a good Muslim is "supposed to do" to himself or herself. He or she is taught this from being a child by his elders and supposed betters: get angry if someone doesn't grovel with respect.

But it's nonsense!

If everyone learned this one simple truth, wars would become a thing of the past.

Marriages and friendships would be saved. A wife could not complain her husband is a beast and abuses her, because he would know his wife is not the reason he flies into rages—he's the one causing it. Beating her up does not quiet his troubled heart (which he knows deep inside).

You can follow this line of reasoning with many examples of your own.

One of my pupils likens her response to tricky grammar questions to "locked-in syndrome", where the unfortunate patient is fully conscious but paralyzed and cannot move a muscle. This lady freezes up and can't think clearly. Grammar does that to her, she believes. But of course she does it to herself, every time a tricky grammar issue arises.

Not Convinced? ··

Some people find this axiomatic truth too much to take on board. But look, here's the clincher: if you decide not to get angry in a given situation, does the anger happen anyway? If you decide not to let your hackles rise and start shouting, can the other party still make you feel angry anyway? Can it be laid on you without your cooperation; something that's "in the air"? Of course not.

You have to create the anger within. It's a choice and not, as some people act, an obligation! Just dump it. Don't do it.

Doc Childre's *HeartMath®Institute* give out a great stopper technique they call the "Freeze-Frame". Everyone should learn to do it, until having sufficient Punk Psychology™ piloting starts to dial back reckless and unwanted emotions.

Freeze Frame® is a one-minute technique that allows a major shift in perception. More than positive thinking, it creates a definitive, heart-felt shift in how we view a situation, an individual or ourselves. When under stress:

Shift out of your head, and focus on the area around your heart. Keep your attention there for at least ten seconds. Continue to breathe normally.

Recall a positive time or feeling you had in your life, and attempt to re-experience it. Remember, try not simply to visualize it, but rather to feel it fully (sensate awareness).

Ask a question from the heart: "What can I do in this situation to make it different?" or "What can I do to minimize stress?"

Listen to the response of your heart.

You may hear nothing, but perhaps feel calmer. The important learning is that we may not have much control over events around us. But we do have control over our emotional response to those events.

Parental Duty

I think it's a massive duty of parents to teach their kids this simple truth and make sure that they grow up strong in the belief that emotions are OK, and safe to play with, provided you control them yourself and don't blame other people!

Naturally, being able to manage your emotions would lead to a better life experience. But somehow the myth has arisen that we are supposed to suffer (probably priest-inspired nonsense). If we don't suffer horribly we are "unfeeling" and robots.

But all that tripe is laid in its proper grave by the scientific fact that happiness is physiologically sound for us; we flourish biologically.

Conversely, when we suffer bad emotions and low mood, we tear up our body, immune system and cells; we get disease; we fall sick and even die (cancer, heart attack, etc.)

An interesting study led to the finding that practicing the Freeze Frame technique described above increased serum IgA levels (a simple but reliable measure of immune response) by as much as 240 percent.

So the nonsense belief—which sadly is still almost universal—that we somehow need, or are better off for, negative emotions, is easily disproved. It can be objectively shown to be dangerously false, by means of blood tests, heart rate variability monitors, psychological profiles and so on!

Love, Gratitude and Forgiveness ....

Something else our PCs need to get a grasp on, before worrying too much about fixing up their memories, is to teach them love, gratitude and forgiveness. Many people are starved for all three. That's no kind of life!

The sad thing about this deficit is that it is completely easy to fix. The person does it for him or her self. No-one else is needed. You can love yourself unconditionally. But it is a learned skill. He or she needs to be shown what to do and watched until it becomes second nature.

The most powerful healing of all comes from forgiveness. The person simply has to let go of the victim modality, look-what-you-did-to-me, I want justice, kind of thinking. This is essential to progress for one very simple reason: being a victim doesn't work! You suffer but it does no good! Trying to make others feel wrong or feel guilty is a fool's game.

It stems usually from the silly notion that forgiveness is somehow "letting the other person off." The truth is, it is releasing the victim from further suffering. It is totally irrelevant whether or not the supposed perpetrator escapes justice!

Love is equally powerful. We need to learn to love more. But most people are stuck on the similarly unworkable computation that "If he or she loves me more, I can love back more." It's the wrong way round. You can find more love by first loving others more.

It's just an act of faith that if you go around manifesting love, you will find more love. It's totally true. But until he or she makes the shift, there is little hope of an individual finding that precious feeling of worth.

One of the major barriers we encounter is that people have little love (or forgiveness) for the Self. He or she is a tragically bad at self respect. But the truth is that it is very hard to love someone who does not love themselves, or even hates themself. You have to love and honor the Self, before others will love and honor you!

Again, self-deprecation, humiliation and unworthiness are taught by the priest classes, because it keeps people in line and needing redemption!

These unhappy traits can be rectified by my own *Love, Gratitude and Forgiveness* tracks on the Kasina device or similar. Slow theta meditation, being walked through important changes of attitude, eventually bring the person to a better place.

We can also do pen-and-paper hacks, such as listing reasons to love and so forth. One of the best pen-and-paper exercizes, however, is to do a gratitude journal...

Gratitude Journal

Each day and every day, at the end of the day, list at least three things that happened which you are grateful for. It seems simple enough. But studies show this is incredibly healing and cheering.

As I wrote for my own multi-media meditation, gratitude brings to mind the good, the positive, the loving, the healing and the many, many beautiful things we have to experience.

It puts down the monster of greed and status. *To be grateful is to affirm, absolutely, that what you have is sufficient and nourishing.*

Gratitude brings you in to the NOW, so that you are not regretting the past and not anxious about the future or wanting things to come into your life.

Gratitude says that my life is rich and I am blessed. It would be nice to have a choir of heavenly angels around to sing this richness to you, every day—but fortunately, this isn't essential! Declaring gratitude for yourself will focus your mind on good things. And you know what they say... that which you focus on comes into your life.

So as well as being grateful for what you have now, you will become richer and richer. Gratitude brings more gratitude!

No one's life is so poor that there is not some cause for celebration.

Teach your cases to think often on this: gratitude speaks of love; it is a song to yourself. Love yourself enough to be very glad for the many, many good and beautiful things in your life. It is your expression of your love for life; it's your connection to all those good things that you celebrate.

Spread this notion as if it were a scripture.

Punk Points: ···

- You have to create emotions within. It's a choice and not, as some people think and act, an obligation! Just dump the habit. Encourage others around you to do the same. Educate your clients to monitor and control their own emotions.

- *Please, I beg you, teach this important truth to any kids who come into your sphere.* It could save them years of misery in times to come.

- Love, gratitude and forgiveness are great tools for overriding the usual obsession with obnoxious emotions.

- The HeartMath Freeze Frame® technique is worth learning and practicing, at least as a temporary tool. Fortunately for us, piloting, over time, gradually erodes the need to indulge in unwanted and inappropriate moods. Indeed, that is one of the main benefits of piloting!

- Get plenty! Piloting will change EVERYTHING about you and your world for the better.

CHAPTER 23

WHERE DO I GO FROM HERE?

If you have read this far, you might be asking yourself the obvious question: where do I go from here?

You need to connect with like-minded souls. You need to join with us. For one thing, membership of our pilot practitioner circle gives you a considerable degree of legal protection. Incredibly, there are people out there who won't like you producing miracle transformations. It will show them up as inept and, rather than improving their act, the will try to attack you and bring you down.

Membership of a club like ours gives you the equivalent freedom of a license, providing the client is also a club member. That's not difficult to arrange.

Plus, you will get torrents of up-to-date information and advice, as research continues.

Most importantly, you will want to develop your skills. Once you have saved a couple of lives, repaired a long-dead marriage and put someone back on the road to prosperity or fame, you will want to know what else can be done!

The Professional Route

If you are ready, you need to join with us and learn more. For starters, you need to become a professional pilot. It's a new career. You will be able to charge significant fees for your interventions. If you are already a health practitioner or life coach, this will add considerably to your bottom line.

You can make contact here: info@supernoetics.com

Among the many things you learn in the professional pilot's course are:

Biofeedback Monitoring ••••••••••••••••••••••••••••••••••••••

Skill in using and interpreting our biofeedback instruments, particularly the galvanic skin-response (GSR) meter.

This device is important in that it shows us where the charge lies. It takes all the guesswork out of what to pilot. In my book *Medicine Beyond* I likened this to "GPS for the mind™" (a term trademarked by my friend and colleague Hank Levin, in respect of his InnerTrac GSR meter).

Basically, if an episode has available charge, it will show a helpful meter response and can be run. If there is no read, we leave it alone, at least for the time being. At a later date, an episode or topic may become "live", and we can then start to deal with it. This avoids the hubris of thinking we know more about what is wrong than the client.

Nothing is more odious to us, as experts, to see inept practitioners insist that an individual dive into early life abuse, or some shocking life trauma that has resulted in PTSD, just because the practitioner "knows" this is what's wrong. That may be true (maybe not) but unless the person is able to cope with looking inwardly at such an awful event, he or she cannot rise above it, break free of the charge and erase it.

Skilled use of a GSR meter is pivotal for this reason.

Moreover, there is a quantitative element to GSR metering. If we see a great deal of meter action (*differential*, we call it) then we know the outcome has been good. This is invariably accompanied by the client reporting they feel "lighter, freer, cleaner, etc."

One final detail, the meter will also tell us that charge has gone from a particular event or topic. In other words, leave well alone. It's done. To keep going lands us in the corny error of dealing with something that is no longer there!

Structured Conversations ··································

We teach you a charge-stripping technique called "structured conversations", so called because it is a series of detailed questions that can be used to rip up charge in any area of a person's life. It's unlimited, so when you have brought about a major recovery on the subject of, say, childhood abuse, you can do it all over again on the topic of work and career (same list or a different list). Then marriage, then a health issue, and so on.

One structured conversation we have nicknamed The Yapper, because it gets a person talking freely, and in depth, about any selected topic. It pulls off charge and negative energies by the bucketload.

You could, factually, create a whole coaching career, just using this one tool!

Talking To Someone Who Isn't There! ···················

This is not a sign of madness. Rather, it is an outgrowth of the fact that two people do not need to be together to have a meaningful dialogue. Indeed, one of them may be dead, so it would be impossible to have a discussion in the material world. It's something that is generated in the client's psychic space (under guidance, of course).

As we all know, it often happens that one party to a difficult relationship won't cooperate in seeking a resolution. Blaming that person doesn't really solve anything, so that's not a smart approach, even though it's the norm. But imagining a fully-developed conversation with him or her can move mountains of charge from a client. He or she typically knows what the other person is thinking and can create a meaningful conversation, leading to a workaround of ideas.

And you know what's magic? The other person seems to respond positively afterwards. Not always but sometimes it's as if that imaginary conversation really took place in the material world, not just in someone's imagination!

We call this hurrah* our "Identity Dialogue" technique. You learn to have a person create any imaginary conversation between themselves and another "person of interest". It can be a lost love, a dead child, even an imaginary creature, provided that makes sense in the context. I've had a client do it with God (shades of Neale Donald Walsch!), to gain extra insight and traction.

Using this imaginary conversation approach, you can heal old relationships, prosper new ones, free a person from loss, guilt or regret and help him or her gain insight into old and difficult encounters, which have since festered in the back of the mind.

[* Hurrah: a Supernoetics® term for an exciting hack or technique that ends with a person feeling really good]

Black and White Technique

Then we can introduce to you another brilliant hack, developed by Ron Fitch in Alameda. It's a way of transforming psychic energies from dark and negative to pure and "clean".

It's great for pain of all kinds. You can also use to eliminate dark mental masses, fatigue, unwanted energies and unpleasant physical sensations. It takes only a matter of minutes to change how a person feels.

What's really cool is that, although it borders on magic, almost anyone can learn to do this hack in less than an hour.

It's finished off with what we call an "energy draw". It's like using a two-by-four pull through (as for cleaning a rifle). It clears "blockages" and allows energy channels to flow freely. Remember, all pain is a blocked flow of some kind. Even spiritual pain can be a blockage of communication. Indeed, usually it is.

The Golden Path ···

The concept of our "Golden Path" is that of a self-growth highway, that we step onto and then just walk (rather like Dorothy's instructions for the yellow-brick road!) It starts humbly, in familiar territory, but takes us further and further afield, into new pathways and pastures.

It's terrific fun actually and very empowering. We have stages along the way, like the repair of former practices and techniques (meditation, EST, psychoanalysis, whatever), a milestone we label "communication enabled" and another for shifting what we call "stubborn self-serving computations" (I'm right and everybody else is WRONG! kind of thinking).

Best of it is when psychic abilities start to develop seriously, with skills in telepathy, travels out of the body and remote viewing. Once entering the stage we call Extreme Mysticism™, an individual begins to definitely see the material universe as something less dense (more and more transparent) and visions in the spiritual realm (without being woo-woo) become more and more real and enjoyable.

Please don't dismiss this as raving. Someone has to go there. Why not me? I've made my name as a relentlessly enquiring medical explorer and a fearless communicator who is not shy about speaking out!

Let me post an article from *Scientific American* in my defense. The voice is that of Francis Crick (he of DNA fame) and younger Christof Koch, an American neuroscientist and professor at Cal-Tech:

"For many years after [William] James penned *The Principles of Psychology* (1890)... most cognitive scientists ignored consciousness, as did almost all neuroscientists. The problem was felt to be either purely "philosophical" or too elusive to study experimentally... In our opinion, such timidity is ridiculous."

Crick, F.H.C. & Koch, C. (1992) The problem of consciousness, *Scientific American*, 267(3), 153-159.

They were, however, far too timid to do what I have attempted to do, not from cowardice, but to protect their status and academic reputation. Nevertheless, they lit a beacon and I would like to keep the flame alight! I have no academic reputation to worry about protecting!

Learning What To Do vs. Cleaning Your Inner Mirror

There are two main ways to start to conquer life. One is to learn more about how things work and so develop tactics and strategies to bring you what you want. The other is to raise your game, through personal exploration and removing inner blockages, resulting in new powers and exceptional abilities.

We do both very well in Supernoetics®!

It needs to be emphasized that there is far more on offer than entry-level Punk Psychology™. Powerful as it is, there are limitations. But these have been more than adequately solved by decades of subsequent research and developments.

The full body of knowledge now known as Supernoetics® is formidable indeed. We truly have *the protocols for change and human transformation*™. There is a large body of learning that would come under the heading of life skills, expertise, or success tactics and strategies. These range from educational and learning principles, to financial powers, through healing, justice, organizing and personal efficiency, to social and political reform and community functionality.

It's often taught that fear is what holds individuals back from success. We say this is gross nonsense, taught by inept wannabe gurus. *It's not knowing what to do or how to go about it that holds people back*. Think about it: if you knew exactly how to create a million-dollar business, step by step, do you think you would be scared to tackle the project? Seriously? You more likely couldn't wait to get started on your dream and would leap out of bed in the morning, to get down to it!

The fear theory degrades people, makes them small and incapable. The ignorance model empowers people because it says, in effect, you are great—you can do anything—all you need is the knowhow, which can easily be learned.

We have that knowledge... in spades!

Then, as well as the body of life skills, we have probably the most powerful human transformation techniques ever devised. That's no idle boast. This is way beyond psychology and into whole new zones of Being and consciousness. We have hundreds of hacks, hurrahs and rubrics to utterly change a person's thinking, from dysfunctional behaviors and emotional ineptitude to soaring psychic powers, beyond the "laws" of current science.

We know where the damage comes from. We know how to discharge and lift its origins (you now know a little about that, having learned Punk Psychology™). Whether you believe in past lives or not, you must be aware than you are part of a thinking commonality, an archetype, if you like, that has bought into the idea that we are a brain, just meat, and then we die, we vanish.

That's not true. You live on in some form or another. As I wrote in my paradigm-shifting book *Medicine Beyond*, advanced physics doesn't just say that awesome things could happen; it says they *must* happen. Like life after death. We, as creatures, are a bundle of energy and information. That information and energy cannot simply vanish because we "die". We continue in some form or another. We are a part of the collective conscious.

So, even if you are not comfortable with re-incarnation, real (honest) physics says you can't just disappear! We must survive as energy and information. Perhaps that's why we sometimes get the feeling of "stepping on someone's grave". We walked into an energy and information field that was once a person!

The dead remain with us. We are a cumulative phenomenon! The poet Homer, Buddha, Jesus and the Prophet Mohammed are here with us now, in every sense, though their physical carcasses rotted away long ago. If you know the Supernoetics® *Twelve Channels of Being* you would say that our Channel Ten is continuously enriched!

The point is, you must be committed to the truth, in whatever form it shows up. If you want someone else to think for you and tell you how the world works, you will remain forever in the grip of the common hysteria. You will be uncomfortably stuck on the horns of a dichotomy, imposed on you by limited thinking: right and wrong, true or not true, left-wing right-wing, possible impossible, and the entire gamut of limitations that Aristotle's logic system creates for us.

In the end, it's ruinous. It means you can't have good without bad, you can't have beauty without creating ugliness, you cannot suppose a God without creating the Devil in tow.

Consciousness, as master of reality, crafts a different experience altogether. Dreams are not just dreams; they are experiences in a different level of reality. Life and death are a question of viewpoint and perspective, not dependent on the breathing of a flesh creature. Past, present and future are *creations*, not mathematical realities.

It is now generally accepted by intelligent scientists (the ones who can think for themselves) that there are, indeed, many universes. Hard core math predicts at least 10^{500} probable universes (that's a 10, followed by 500 zeroes!), each with different laws of physics. As cosmologist Alexander Vilenkin of Tufts University, has been quoted as saying, "I have never been happy with the idea that there are an infinite number of Alexander Vilenkins out there. Unfortunately, I think it is likely to be true."

So, are you ready for the great adventure? Are you ready—truly—for what the mind will reveal to you, once you release its amazing powers?

Life Beyond The Brain

In the Introduction to this book, I posited the extended mind (beyond the brain) model. For some, who would rather sit comfortably in the middle of a solid, material universe in which humans have no active role, that is challenging concept.

But to hold that just-a-brain view it is necessary to ignore a great deal of human experience and ignoring what's going on is never a good way to the truth!

More and more people are familiar with the territory outside of time and space, where deep connections take place. Few people these days do not believe in at least some psi phenomena (telepathy, telekinesis, remote viewing, etc.)

In May 2000, the *New York Times Sunday Magazine* published results of a poll conducted by Blum & Weprin Associates; a disproportionate 81% said they believed in life after death.

According to a 2001 Gallup poll, 75% of Americans hold at least one paranormal belief (41% believe in extrasensory perception, or ESP, 37%

believe that houses can be haunted and 32% believe that ghosts/the spirits of dead people can come back in certain places or situations). A UK newspaper poll showed that 60% of Britons accept the existence of the paranormal.

An online research poll conducted in 2006 by Australian researchers, and was answered by some 2,000 people, revealed a whopping 96% of respondents claim to have had at least one brush with the paranormal. Results showed that 70% of respondents believe an unexplained event changed their lives, mostly in a positive way. Some 70% also claim to have seen, heard, or been touched by an animal or person that wasn't there; 80% report having had a premonition; and almost 50% recalled a previous incarnation.

Are all these individuals demented or deluded, as current science would claim? Or is it that absurd mechanistic science has simply got it wrong and is refusing to look at phenomena that are clear as day and calling out to be properly (and honestly) investigated?

Sir Roger Penrose, an English mathematical physicist, philosopher of science and Professor of Mathematics at Oxford University thinks so:

"A scientific world-view which does not profoundly come to terms with the problem of conscious minds can have no serious pretensions of completeness. Consciousness is part of our universe, so any physical theory which makes no proper place for it falls fundamentally short of providing a genuine description of the world. I would maintain that there is yet no physical, biological, or computational theory that comes very close to explaining our consciousness ... "

Roger Penrose, *Shadows Of The Mind*. OUP 1994.

Yet we are in a system which says we are a blob and that's all there is to being: just blobbery! Nothing exists beyond the physical. There are no pretensions to higher, non-material phenomena. The paranormal is an outrageous delusion. Why? Because it can't be true, says science. More like "it mustn't be true," really. There is a sort of desperation to exclude the higher life. The trouble for these dyed-in-the-wool reductionist thinkers is that if they admit even just one tiny phenomenon that doesn't fit with their supposed laws of physics, then the whole of science collapses.

Reality can't then be the way they are describing it. So it's an all-or-nothing dilemma they find themselves in. There isn't... there mustn't be... anything paranormal.

Fortunately, however, at least the American Psychiatric Association's Diagnostic and Statistical Manual of Mental Disorders (DSM) has now been amended so that genuinely psychic people are no longer considered "disordered"!

Helping Others

Well, this is a lot to take in. One of the questions you must ask yourself is: *do I want to know more, do more and BE more?*

Then follows the decision whether helping others conquer their limitations has meaning for you. If not, that's fine. Not everyone is a Samaritan. People have careers, family, commitments and established routines.

But if you really want to help us take on the ambitious project of "working for the purposeful re-invention of Mankind™" then join us.

You can make contact via: info@supernoetics.com

Certainly, the world needs help right now. As intellects shrivel before the onslaught of globalist and Big Business propaganda, people retreat more and more into social media, whole nations polarize in a frightening, almost savage, intolerance of anyone with different views, and small groups try to destroy whatever they object to with their cruel and violent agendas, one could be forgiven for thinking the world cannot go on for long, deteriorating as it is.

Something needs to change. And that something is not a new president or new king, not a new political agenda, not new and oppressive laws "for the common good", not a newer and better Facebook algorithm or a new internet platform. Electric cars, smartphone tracking apps, wearable health monitors, soft AI, G5 telephones, nano-computers, or any other so-called disruptive technology, just won't cut it.

The problem is the human mind and not enough has been done to try to come to terms with it and how to modify it to the person's benefit.

Here at least we have made a significant start. The result is not an automated, robot-like human, or rows of identical plastic dolls; we do not produce Pavlovian-trained animals, that respond only to stimuli and have no personal dreams. Rather, we free the spirit, releasing it to be whatever it wants to be.

And if you haven't thought about it before, that's a very large universe out there (or many of them), and an almost infinite range of possibilities for the unfettered mind!

"We

are participators in bringing into being not only the near and here but the far away and long ago."

John Wheeler, American physicist, 2006.

Made in the USA
Lexington, KY
03 May 2018